Social Security for the Elderly

Edited by
R.K.A. Subrahmanya

SHIPRA

ISBN 81-7541-219-4

Social Security for the Elderly

First Published in India in 2005

Published by :
SHIPRA PUBLICATIONS
115-A, Vikas Marg, Shakarpur,
Delhi-110092 (India)
Ph. : 91-11-55277210, 22500954
Email : siprapub@satyam.com.in
Website : shiprapublications.com

Laser Typesetting by :
R.S. Prints,
New Delhi

Printed at :
Chaudhary Offset,
Delhi-110006

Contents

Preface

Issues concerning social security for the elderly were debated at a seminar held in Delhi, in which China, India, Pakistan, Sri Lanka and Nepal participated and certain broad conclusions were reached. The relvant papers are contained in this book.

The organizers are thankful to Shipra Publications for agreeing to publish the book.

It is hoped that the readers will find the volume useful and rewarding

R. K. A. Subrahmanya
Secretary General,
Social Security Association of India

Bangalore

1

Introduction

R.K.A.Subrahmanya

Social security is the security provided by the society to the vulnerable groups of people consisting of young children, the elderly, the sick, the disabled and those who become vulnerable due to unemployment or otherwise. Of these the elderly represent a large and growing group. Their vulnerability increases with age and they become more and more dependant on other people.

Traditionally, the elderly persons were looked after by the younger members of the family to which they belonged. With the breaking up of the joint family systems and the advent of new ways of life the family ties are weakening and it has become necessary for the States and societies to assume responsibility for the care of the elderly. Social security for the elderly is therefore gaining increasing importance.

One can have an idea of the pitiable condition of the elderly from the following data collected in the course of a study in UP[1] :

75 per cent suffer from physical disability
60 per cent face a great sense of alienation
48 per cent are extremely lonely
46 per cent face economic problems
40 per cent feel unwanted by their children
35 per cent feel that no one cares for them
33 per cent are unhappy that there is lack of respect from the members of the family
33 per cent are worried about bad health
52 per cent have no one to help them to do their work including cooking of their meals
67 per cent feel that their family treats them with contempt
25 per cent suffer from depression
12 per cent have no hope of economic support from any source. 10 per cent suffer from a sense of economic alienation.

The social security needs of the elderly are therefore varied. Lonely old people are routinely assaulted and sometimes killed for their money They need protection against physical assault by unscrupulous elements. The police have established helplines for helpless people to contact them in case of need.

The old by definition have retired form work and they can no longer earn their livelihood. They therefore need income security or an arrangement under which their basic needs are met. They are prone to all kinds of ailments. They therefore need health security.

Above all they feel lonely and are prone to depression, dementia and other kinds of mental diseases. They need someone to help them do their routine jobs such as paying bills etc. and to keep them in good humour by giving them company and talking to them.

Globally there is an increasing awareness of the problems of the aged. Two World Assemblies have been held to discuss those problems and to draw up plans for dealing with those problems. Many countries have also adopted national policies for the elderly.

In India the National Policy on Older Persons was adopted in 1999. The National Policy "seeks to assure older persons that their concerns are national concerns and they will not live unprotected, ignored, or marginalized. The goal of the National Policy is the well being of older persons. It aims to strengthen their legitimate place in society and help older persons to live the last phase of their life with purpose dignity and peace.

"The Policy visualizes that the State will extend support for financial security, health care, shelter, welfare and other needs of older persons, provide protection against abuse and exploitation, make available opportunities for development of the potential of older persons, seek their participation and provide services so that they can improve the quality of their lives."[2]

Demography of Ageing

The most basic problem of the elderly lies in the growth of numbers. The number of the elderly has been growing both in terms of absolute numbers and also as a percentage of the total population. all over the world especially in the developing countries. India and China account for a significant proportion of the growing numbers.

The percentage of the elderly in the world population is expected to grow from 9.5 in 1995 to 20.7 in 2050 and to 30.5 in 2150. In absolute numbers the elderly are expected to increase from 542 million in 1995 to 1.9 billion in 2050 and 3.3 billion in 2150. In India the population of the elderly is expected to grow from 71 million in 2001 to 179 million in 2011 and further to 301 million by 2050.

There are two reasons for this growth; first, there is a general growth of population due to high rate of fertility; and second, the longevity of the population has been rising and therefore people are living longer than they used to do in the past.

According to the report of *Human Development in South Asia 1997*:

> "The rapidly increasing population in South Asian countries poses one of the key challenges to human development in the region. The population has more than doubled in the last three decades from 563 million in 1960 to 1191 million in 1993. This population is expected to double again over the next 25 years. According to the long range UN projections, the total population of South Asia will be staggering 2.8 billion in 2050. India would have surpassed China by then to become the most populous country in the world. With a population of 1.7 billion."

Can the growth of the numbers be checked? The answer is yes and no as well.

The general growth of population can be checked provided the countries adopt and implement effective population control policies. According to the report of *Human Development in South Asia 1997*:

> "In the final analysis, a determined effort to reduce population growth must start with a firm political commitment. Among the positive steps which must be taken are greater acceleration in the education of girls and women, better provision of reproductive health facilities and incentives for smaller families through a faster pace of economic development."

In India there has been family planning or family welfare policy since Independence. Reduction in the population growth rate is the objective of the policy. It has also been recognized as one of the priority objectives of the five year plans. For various reasons this objective has not been fully achieved. The annual exponential population growth rate in India has been over 2 per cent in the last three decades. The growth rate during the year 1991-2001 was however 1.93 per cent. This compares with the world average of 1.4 per cent and the Chinese growth rate of 1 per cent. The National Population Policy aims at achieving a stable population by 2045. The medium term objective of the Policy is to bring down the Total Fertility rate to the replacement level of 2.1 per cent by 2010. It would therefore appear that there would be no prospect of any significant reduction in the rate of growth of the population in the near future in India.

According to the National Policy on Older Persons :

> "Expectation of life at birth for males has shown a steady rise from 42 years in 1951–60 to 58 years in 1986-90; it is projected to be 67 years in 2011–16, an increase of about 9 years in a twentyfive year period (1986-90 to 2011-16). In the case of females, the increase in expectation of life has been higher — about 11years during the same period, from 58 years in 1986-90 to 69 years in 2011-16. At age 60 too, the expectation of life shows a steady rise and is a little higher for women. In 1989 -93 it was 15 years for males and 16 years for females."[3]

(According to *Economic Survey, 2001–2002*, life expectancy at birth had already reached 60.4 in case of males and 61.8 in case of females.)

> "Improved life expectancy has contributed to an increase in the number of 60+ persons. From only 12 million 60+ persons in India in 1901, the number crossed 20 million in 1951 and 57 million in1991. Population projections (1996) indicate that the 100 million mark is expected to be reached in 2013. Projections beyond 2016 made by the United Nations (1996 revision) has indicated that India will have 198 million 60+ persons in 2030 and 326 million in 2050. The percentage of 60+ persons in the total population has seen a steady rise from 5.1% in 1901 to 6.8% in 1991.It is expected to reach 8.9% in 2016. Projections beyond 2016 made by United Nations (1996 revision) has indicated that 21 percent of the Indian population will be 60+ by 2050."[4]

> "Growth rate on a larger demographic base implies a much larger increase in numbers. This will be the case in coming years."[5]

The rise in longevity is the result of improved conditions of life. As the ultimate object of economic and social development is to improve the conditions of life there can be no reduction in the numbers of persons getting older. Every developing country especially India and China should therefore aim at restricting the general growth of population by implementing population control policies more effectively.

Poverty

The second major problem of the elderly is poverty. The problem of poverty of the elderly also has two dimensions, namely, the level of poverty of the general population and the level of poverty of the elderly in particular.

Table 1.1 : Population below the Poverty Line

Country	National %	International* %
Bangladesh 1995-96	35.6	31.8
China 1998	4.6	21.0
India 1994	35.0	41.4
Nepal 1995-96	42.0	37.5
Pakistan 1991	34.0	35.0
Sri Lanka 1990-91	35.3	13.5

* Poverty gap @US$ 2 a day.
Source: *World Developemnt Report*, 2000–01.

In all the countries, except China, the percentage of people below the poverty line (national) exceeds 30 per cent. A later assessment made in India shows that the percentage of population below the poverty line in 1999-2000 was 26 per cent. In terms of absolute numbers it was 260 million. The percentage of people below the poverty line in the developing countries is much higher than in many of the developed countries. According to the report of *Human Development in South Asia 1997* :

> " in the global context, the South Asian region has begun to lag behind all other regions of the world, both in its income and in human development levels. South Asia is by now the poorest region in the world. Its per capita income of $ 309 is below $ 555 for Sub-Saharan Africa and $ 970 for all developing countries. While its share in world population is 22 percent, it contains nearly 40 percent of the world's absolute poor."

Studies have shown that among the poor the elderly represent the poorest segment of the population. Retirement leads to poverty especially in countries like India. Low or no income is the biggest problem in old age. Many persons have therefore to continue to work even in old age. There is no such thing as retirement for them except in the case of government employees and workers in the organized sector who constitute a small percentage of total workforce. They work practically till death out of need.

The table 1.2[6] shows the work participation rate among the elderly in the age group 65 +

Table 1.2: Work Participation Rate - Age Group 65+, 2000

	Developed		Developing	
	M	F	M	F
Work Participation of the old	17	6	34	10

The Work Participation Rate among the elderly in India in 1991 was as follows[7]:

Table 1.3 : Work Particitation Rate among Eledery in India, 1991

	Rural	Urban	Total
Total	43.10	24.29	39.13
Male	65.36	42.93	60.53
Female	18.96	6.90	16.14

The work participation rate of the females appears to be low because their work is such that it does not enter statistics. Indeed old women work more than old men.

According Kumudini Dandekar: "In 1971 among those aged 60 and above, more than three fourths of the rural population worked; this proportions fell to two thirds in 1981. In urban areas more than half (55%) worked after 60 years of age in 1971 and 48 percent in 1981."

Those who do not work have to depend on their children. Even those who work cannot be said to be totally independent. It is said that nearly 70 per cent of the elderly in India live with their children contributing to their expenses and less than 20% live on their pensions independently.

Dandekar says: "Poverty or inadequacy of income leads to dependence on children in old age. For those with land to cultivate, the son can be relied upon; others have to depend on their own labour or that of their children. It is not enough for one's own children as well as the old parents. Moreover, poverty in India is so severe that people tend to live from day to day earnings. Incomes are inadequate to meet the two responsibilities of raising children and taking care of aging parents."

She has pointed out that with gradual fall in the birth rate the dependency load of rearing children will decrease but that of providing for the old will increase. The total dependency ratio in 2001 according to her was 59.6 which was expected to go up to 70.8 by 2081 as shown in Table 1.4:

Table 1.4: Dependency Ratio

Year	0-14/15-59	60+/15-59	Total dependency
2001	55.7	11.9	67.6
2011	46.6	13.0	59.6
2021	40.0	15.7	55.7
2081	34.7	36.1	70.8

Not all the elderly are dependent. A large number of them are economically independent but they have to carry the load of dependence of others. According to Dandekar:

> "In India as a whole 51 percent of men in rural areas and 46 per cent in urban areas were economically independent. Of these 71 per cent, both in rural and urban areas had to carry a load of dependency. In other words, the independent men were still working and were not yet free of responsibilities."

The National Policy on Older Persons in India says that employment in income generating activities after superannuation should be the choice of the individual and it seeks to encourage and support organizations which provide career guidance training, orientation and support services for that purpose. At the same time, the Constitution of India requires that the State should ensure that "citizens are not forced by economic necessity to enter vocations unsuited to their age or strength."[8] It is therefore important that participation of the elderly in any employment should be optional and not necessary. Where a person is not able to work for reasons of age or health there should be appropriate arrangements to provide him the means of livelihood.

Persons who have saved enough money during their active life can invest the money or contribute to a pension scheme and live on the proceeds of such investment, but for others there should be social security.

Financial Security

Social security is broadly of two kinds, namely, income security and health security.

According to the ILO, the object of income security is to "relieve want and prevent destitution by restoring, up to a reasonable level, income which is lost by reason of inability to work, or to obtain remunerative work or by reason of death of the breadwinner."[9] Oldage is one of the contingencies in which income security will be required. Oldage benefit has therefore become an important branch of social security.

Recommendation No. 67 of the ILO concerning Income Security says that "the contingency for which oldage benefit should be paid is the attainment of a prescribed age, which should be that at which persons commonly become incapable of efficient work, the incidence of sickness and invalidity becomes heavy and unemployment, if present is likely to be permanent."

ILO Convention No. 128 concerning Invalidity, Oldage and Survivors' Benefits provides that the prescribed age should be not more than 65 or such other higher age as may be fixed by the competent authority. The recommendations of the ILO further require that income security including oldage benefit should be organized as far as possible on the basis of compulsory social insurance, whereby insured persons fulfilling prescribed qualifying conditions would be entitled, in consideration of the contributions they have made to an insurance institution to benefits payable at specified rates on the occurrence of the specified contingencies and that the benefits should be paid in the form of periodical payments.

In other words persons who have attained the age of 65 or such higher age as may be fixed by the competent authority should be entitled to receive periodical payments sufficient for their subsistence.

There are a variety of social security schemes intended to provide oldage benefit in most of the countries. A study of the world scenario as on 1 January 1995 shows that there were 165 countries which had one or other type of social security programmes. Of these, 158 countries provided oldage, disability and/or survivors benefit in one form or the other. The rest of the seven countries did not have any oldage disability or survivors scheme in operation. The break up of the 158 countries which had oldage disability and /or survivors programme shows the following picture:

Number of countries which had contributory earnings related pension schemes	: 132
Number of countries which had Public Provident Funds	: 19*
Number of countries which had non-contributory means tested systems	: 4
Number of countries which had contributory flat rate systems	: 3

Notes:

* 7 in Asia, 6 in Oceania and 6 in Africa & Australia, Newzealand, South Africa and Hong Kong, Seychelles, Estonia and Netherlands.

Besides, several countries have, in addition to these measures, other systems providing oldage, invalidity and survivors benefits like:

(a) Contributory flat rate schemes for certain categories of employees;
(b) non-contributory—either means tested or flat rate universal schemes; and
(c) mandatory private savings schemes as distinct from public provident fund

In Asia and the Pacific, the situation as on 1 January 1995 was as follows:

Total number of countries in Asia and he Pacific	49
Number of countries which have contributory Earnings related pension schemes	31
Number of countries having public provident funds	13
Number of countries which have non-contributory Means tested pension schemes	3
Number of countries which have no oldage invalidity or survivors benefits	2

Source: Income Security for the Elderly: International Perspective by S.K. Wadhawan, 1996.

Pension Reform

Many of the schemes indicated above would have been introduced out of historical necessity and cannot be said to represent well-conceived policies. Many countries have therefore embarked on reform of the schemes and there is an obvious necessity for such reform.

Coverage

Although there are several schemes to provide oldage benefit in each country, their coverage being small they do not cover all the elderly population.

The ILO appointed a committee on Social Security during the 89th International Labour Conference to consider the issues and challenges facing social security. The committee *inter alia* examined the coverage of social security and observed as follows:

> "A very large proportion of the population in most regions of the world still does not enjoy any social protection or is covered only very partially. This is the case for the vast majority of people in developing countries, and even in some of the richest industrialized countries there are large and growing gaps in social protection.
>
> "Informal economy workers are not covered by social security for a variety of reasons."

With the growth in the numbers of the aged, the gap in coverage of the elderly has been growing.

The Table 1.5 shows the coverage under the various oldage benefit schemes as of 1996:

Table 1.5: Population Coverage Under Old Age Benefit Schemes

Country	Pensioners to total population Per cent	Pensioners to population older than 59 Per cent	Pensioners to population older than 64 Per cent
China	1.9	20.5	31.3
Indonesia	0.1	1.9	3.0
Korea	0.3	3.4	5.4
Malaysia	0.2	4.2	6.4
Pakistan	0.10	2.00	3.29
Sri Lanka	0.94	10.60	15.70
Thailand	0.00	0.01	0.01

(Source: ILO 2000)

In India the existing schemes cover persons in the high income brackets, workers in the organized sector and the destitutes with little or no income of their own. The workers in the unorganized sector who constitute more than 90 per cent of the workforce, and the old people outside the workforce have no pension or provident fund scheme worth mentioning (The LIC has two subsidized insurance schemes called Jana Shree Bima Yojana and Khetihar Mazdoor Bima

Yojana which are basically life insurance schemes but with a pension element. The Government of West Bengal has introduced a subsidized provident scheme for the workers in the unorganized sector. The coverage of these schemes is also small.). People in the rural sector are largely ignored.

The number of persons covered under the Provident Fund and pension schemes in India is less than 5 per cent of the total population.

China has a rural pension scheme but that is a voluntary scheme with provision for a collective subsidy. A voluntary scheme though open to every one cannot be deemed to be universal in application.

In the circumstances there is an ongoing debate on the possibility of introducing a pension system encompassing the entire population of the elderly in each country and several innovative measures are also being tried out for extension of coverage.

The National Pension System in South Korea, for example, which previously covered 7.8 million workers was extended in 1999 to cover a further 8.9 million persons comprising the urban self employed and employees of firms with fewer than five workers.[10]

In Brazil, according to a household survey conducted in 1999, 77.3 percent of those aged 60 or over were receiving benefits from social security institutions including social assistance pensions and public servants funds. The high coverage was reported to be due to two programmes, namely, the Social Assistance Pensions and the Rural Social Security Programme.

Extension of coverage of social security for the elderly, however, involves several questions such as: (a) whether such a system should comprise a single scheme or a combination of several schemes, (b) whether the schemes should be mandatory or voluntary, (c) whether the schemes should be public or private.

In India, the National Policy for Older Persons has proposed the expansion of the coverage under the oldage pension scheme for poor persons with the ultimate aim of covering all older persons below the poverty line It has also proposed to revise the rates of pension periodically so that inflation does not deflate its real purchasing power. It states further that, simultaneously, the public distribution system should reach out to cover all 60+ persons living below the poverty line.

The Second National Commission on Labour has also made similar recommendations: The Commission has recommended that all men and women of the age of 65 and above should be covered under a National Pension Scheme subject to an income test related to the poverty line and paid a pension at an enhanced rate of Rs. 200 per month (current rate Rs. 75 per month fixed in 1995) linked to the cost of living index. It has also recommended review and rationalization of the public distribution system.

The National Policy has also envisaged expansion of the base of pension coverage by facilitating the establishment of pension schemes both in the private as well as in the public sector for self employed and salaried persons in non-governmental employment, with provision for employers also to contribute thereto. In fact after the insurance sector was thrown open to private participation several new insurance companies came into being and they are offering a variety of pension schemes. There are proposals to introduce a pension scheme for the workers in the unorganized sector and to establish a regulatory authority.

The National Commission on Labour has envisaged coverage of the entire population under a comprehensive system of social security comprising of four tiers as follows:

(a) Social assistance programmes, financed from the exchequer and wholly based on tax revenues for the absolute poor who cannot make any contribution;

(b) schemes which are partly contributory and partly subsidized by the State for workers in the unorganized sector who can make some contribution but not the entire amount and who being self-employed, have no employers or, being employed on casual basis have no regular employer who can make contribution on a continuing basis;

(c) wholly contributory social insurance schemes for workers in the organized sector; and

(d) voluntary schemes for those who can make their own provision.

The first three tiers will be mandatory but the last one will be voluntary.

An alternative to the recommendation of the Commission would be to have a mandatory universal basic pension scheme covering the entire population which could be tax based or contributory, as the case may be, which may be supplemented by one or more schemes which would be contributory on a voluntary basis for those who wish to supplement the basic pension and can make necessary contributions therefrom.

Whatever be the means of extension of coverage, it is likely to add to the cost of social security unless compensatory measures are adopted. It is necessary and possible to adopt appropriate measures to cope with this problem.

Pension Versus Provident Fund

As already pointed out, the Recommendation No. 67 of the ILO concerning income security requires that the oldage benefit should be preferably in the form of periodical payments, that is, pensions. But many countries in Asia and Africa have opted for provident fund schemes which provide for lump sum payments. Provident funds are basically savings schemes and they do not insure the subscribers against any risks. They do not involve any pooling or sharing of risks. The benefits are strictly proportional to the contributions made and therefore they are regarded as defined contribution schemes. It is however open to the subscribers to purchase annuities from an insurance company on receipt of lump sum amounts from a provident fund organisation.

There is lately a trend for conversion of provident funds into pension schemes. In India the Employees Provident Fund was partially converted into a pension scheme in 1996 but this conversion has not been acceptable to all workers. Some trade union organizations have challenged the decision in the courts and the matter is currently in the Supreme Court.

The preference for provident funds against pensions arises for several reasons. Firstly, administration of provident fund schemes is easier than pension schemes. It is therefore said that provident funds are more common among less developed countries. Secondly, some subscribers to the provident fund believe that if they get lump sum amounts after their retirement they can make better investment than a pension authority and earn better return and better income than what a pension scheme can give. There was some validity in this thinking when the rates of interest were high in India. With the general fall in the interest rates and prospective further fall people are losing confidence in being able to make better investments. Thirdly, if a person receives a lump sum benefit and is able to make a good investment it could be passed on to his successors in case of his early death where as the pension payable under a pension scheme would cease on his death. Where the age of retirement is high and the life expectancy low a person may not be able to draw pension for long and the investment in a pension scheme may turn out to be a loss unless there is provision for a family pension or return of capital. Many pension schemes do therefore make such provisions by reducing the rates of pension In case a person lives long a pension scheme may be more beneficial. Fourthly, provident funds provide better protection than pension against inflation unless the pensions are protected against inflation, because if a person gets a lump sum amount and invests in the stock market he gets the advantage of market capitalization which more than compensates for the loss of value due to inflation. A pension may also be protected against inflation if it is linked to the cost of living index, but few pension schemes are so linked. Lastly, a provident fund scheme may be better even from the point of view of the contributors because under such a PF scheme the rates of contribution will be fixed whereas a pension scheme, if it is based on a defined benefit scheme, the rates of contribution may have to be adjusted from time to time in order to ensure that the pensioners receive the assured benefit increase.

The arguments against a provident fund scheme are mainly two. Firstly, a person who receives a lump sum amount will have the temptation to fritter it away on conspicuous consumption of inessential things and may not have enough money to invest for future earnings. In fact, it is well known that many provident funds have liberal withdrawal provisions so that the subscribers are able to withdraw the balances in the PF account for various purposes and the amounts available for investment when a person retires would be very small and its investment would not yield any significant income during oldage. Suggestions to de-liberalise the premature withdrawal provisions in the schemes have met with resistance from trade union leaders. Secondly, assuming that a person is prudent enough not to withdraw the amounts in the PF prematurely it is doubtful if he will be able to make a sound investment of the lump sum amounts received at the end of his service ensuring the safety and liquidity of the capital as well as a high return on the investment.

Choice between provident fund and pension scheme is therefore difficult.

Public or Private Pension Funds

Social security by definition consists of public measures introduced by the State by legislation or otherwise and administered and also to a large extent financed by the State. Lately, opinion is gaining ground that it should better be left to private initiative.

In India, the Ministry of Social Justice which is said to have been entrusted with the nodal responsibility for older persons had appointed a committee to make recommendations for a future pension system in India. The Committee has expressed the opinion that the issues of ageing, health and income security during oldage etc should be addressed through thrift and self-help, where people prepare for oldage by savings accumulating through their decades in the labour force. The role of the State is to create the necessary infra-structure to enable and encourage each citizen to undertake this task. It has recommended specifically that "the new pension system should be based on individual retirement account. An individual should create this account, have a pass book, where he can see a balance that is his notional wealth at that point in time; he should control how this wealth is managed; this account should stay with his regardless of where he is or where he works. He would make contributions towards his pension into this account through his working life and obtain benefits from it after retirement for the rest of his life."[11]

It is envisaged that the new pension system would be operated by several insurance companies and that it would generate large amounts of money and therefore the Government would have to set up a regulatory authority instead of implementing the pension schemes directly.

There is nothing wrong in promoting thrift and encouraging people to make contributions to a pensions scheme for their income security during oldage, but the question is whether all the workers would be able to make adequate contributions to ensure adequate income during oldage. Historically social security came into being in a situation where the workers being absorbed in their struggle for existence had neither the ability nor the motivation to save for the future. That situation has not changed. The individual retirement accounts cannot therefore provide income security to the workers especially those below or near the poverty line. It can at best be a supplementary scheme whereby persons in the middle and the higher income groups may be able to invest their savings and earn additional pension it cannot take the place of a universal basic pension scheme.

Lately, the publicly managed social security pensions schemes are being criticised for being responsible for the profligacy of the State and misallocation of national resources. There is therefore a demand for a review of the oldage income security arrangements with a suggestion to transfer the management of pension funds to the private sector on the ground that it will be more efficient.

An ADB sponsored study of the Employees Provident Funds Scheme and the Employees Pension Scheme in India has mooted the idea that the management of EPF funds should be outsourced "to private accredited fund managers under liberalised investment guidelines and appropriate regulatory oversight."

It appears, however, that the demand for privatisation of pension funds is motivated by commercial interest. The principal argument in favour of private management of pension schemes is that private managers can obtain better investment returns. This argument is questionable in the context of the various scams and scandals that have to come to light in the working of the money markets, especially in Asia, and the experience of mutual funds in India. There is therefore a great deal of scepticism about it and it is being opposed particularly by organised labour.

There is no dispute about the efficiency of private management but it depends largely on the free play of market forces. In a state of imperfect competition whether a private management can function as effectively and successfully is a moot question. Where the money market is subject to violent fluctuations, people in the lower rungs of society are apt to have greater faith in the State than in private management. There is therefore no escape for the Governments to run the schemes. Private management may be attractive to the middle class self-employed persons with better means. But it is unlikely to be acceptable to persons who cannot afford to take risks with their hard-earned savings.

In the circumstances any arrangement under which people will be able to make their own arrangements for income security in oldage should be welcome as it will reduce the burden on the State but the State, cannot be absolved of the responsibility to provide social security especially for those classes of people who are excluded from the growth process and cannot be left to the care of the market forces.

Age of Retirement

Whatever be the mode of providing income security during oldage there are certain issues common to all of them. One of them is the age of retirement.

The capacity to work dwindles with age and a time comes when every person will have to retire from work. Recommendations of the ILO provide that the age of retirement should not be higher than 65. The actual age of retirement in Asia and the Pacific ranges from 55 to 65 (ILO 2000). In China, Pakistan and Vietnam the normal age of retirement is 60 for men and 55 for women. In Sri Lanka, the normal age of retirement is 55 for men and 50 for women. In India, it is 58 for industrial workers, 60 for Central Government employees, and 65 for judges of the Supreme Court. There is however no age of retirement for workers in the unorganized sector.

The current trend is to raise the pensionable age Enhancement of the age of retirement is one way to provide for oldage so that the young –old will remain at work, continue to contribute to a pension scheme and the burden of the pension system will be lessened. But there is opposition to enhancement of the age of retirement on the ground that the elderly people will deprive or reduce the opportunities for employment and promotion of younger persons.

There is however a strong case for fixing a uniform age of retirement in all cases and raising it from time to time corresponding to the increase in life expectancy by keeping a uniform difference between life expectancy and the age of retirement of say ten or fifteen years corresponding to life expectancy at age 60 or 65 so that the pension system will not have to carry increasing burden due to increasing longevity.

Flat Rate or Earning Related Pensions

Flat rates of pension are fixed without regard to ones service contribution or income on the basis of the basic needs of the pensioners. Universal basic pensions are paid on this basis to all persons who have attained a specified age.

Earning related pensions are paid to persons in employment on the basis of the period of their service or contributions, income and the replacement rate. The schemes provide for a minimum period of service and contributions for a minimum pension and a maximum period of service or contributions for the maximum pension. The actual pension paid would be proportionate to the period of qualifying service or contribution. The schemes specify what types of income are taken into consideration in fixing the rates of pension, for what periods and what percentage of the same is paid as pension. The rate of pension may be based on the last pay drawn, or on the basis of the average pay drawn for different periods such as ten months, one year, three years or for the entire period of service. The rate of pension will be very high if it is based on the last pay drawn. The average for varying periods will tend to reduce it. As contributions to the pensions schemes would have been paid at different rates depending on one's income, payment of pension on the basis of the last pay drawn or on the basis of the average for the last one year or three years the pension paid is likely to be higher than the amount of contributions received. Pension experts therefore recommend taking the average for the entire service as the basis for fixing the rate of pension. Actually however the average is taken for lesser periods such as ten months one year or three years and it affects the viability of the schemes. The replacement rate may be 50% or more. Many pension schemes aim at assuring the pensioner, by themselves or in combination with other schemes even after retirement, the pay last drawn before retirement.

Flat rates of pensions satisfy the primary purpose of social security which is to assure a basic minimum income to every one including the elderly. The pension rates will be low. They can cover much larger persons even where the resources available are limited.

On the other hand earning related pensions aim at maintaining the standard of life of the pensioners and therefore tend to be comparatively very high and it would be difficult to maintain payment of pensions at such high rates especially in times of financial crises Many developed countries had raised the rates of pension when the going was good but they are now experiencing the need for cutting them down. The right approach appears to be to fix the social security pensions at fixed flat rates leaving it to the individuals to supplement them through voluntary scheme.

Funded Pensions and Unfunded Pensions

A pension may be paid on pay-as-you-go basis from the current revenues of the Government or institution as the case may be. Alternatively the contributions received may be placed in a fund and invested in a prescribed manner or in designated securities and pensions may be paid out of the accumulations. In the first case the receipts and payments should be balanced each year. In the second case the balance may be achieved over a period of time depending on several factors including the rate of interest, mortality etc. The rates of contributions and benefits are fixed by the actuaries accordingly taking into account the period within which the pension account needs to be balanced.

Usually the pension schemes based on social assistance are paid on pay-as-you-go basis and the contributory pension schemes are funded.

The Central Government employees in India, on their retirement from service, are paid pension on pay-as-you-go basis from the central exchequer. It is believed that the burden of payment of such pension is growing and it may not be possible to continue to make such payments for long. There is therefore a proposal to convert it into a contributory funded scheme. The proposal is to collect contributions at fixed rates from the employees and to make matching contribution from the government. The new scheme will be effective prospectively and will be applicable to those who will be recruited hereafter. The scheme will have a long gestation period of about 35 years and till then the government will have to pay the existing pensioners and the existing employees on the existing basis and also contribute to the new scheme. The pension burden for the next 35 years or so is likely to be doubled. It is a moot question whether the government will be able to bear that burden.

Besides, it is also a moot question whether the government will be able to discriminate between the existing employees and the new recruits in the matter of pensions. The existing pay structure of the Central Government employees in India is based on the premise that they will be entitled to pension at the cost of the government. If that premise is changed the employees are likely to demand revision of the pay structure involving enhancement of their pay to enable them to contribute to the pension fund so that the principle of equal pay for equal work enshrined in the constitution is not violated.

Defined Contribution or Defined Benefit Schemes

A scheme where the quantum of benefit is defined and the rates of contribution required for ensuring such benefit is variable is called Defined Benefit Scheme. Conversely, a scheme where the rate of contribution is fixed and the quantum of benefits is varied as necessary is called a defined contribution scheme. Schemes which are based on Pay-as-you-go principle are ordinarily defined benefit schemes and the funded schemes are ordinarily defined contribution schemes. The two types of schemes represent the two sides of the market, the supply side and the demand side. Defined benefit schemes are favoured by the demand side while the defined contribution schemes are favoured by the supply side. The current day reformists are on the on the supply side. And they are advocating replacement of all defined benefit schemes by defined contribution schemes. One of the major recommendations of the OASIS report in India is for "a movement to a defined contribution system where a person would get retirement benefits in the form of annuity – regular monthly income – on the basis of pre-defined contributions made from his salary in his lifetime."[12] Such a movement, while it may protect the financial stability of the scheme, is likely to defeat the basic purpose of the scheme, that is, to assure a person of an income required for a decent life.

In this connection it is relevant to point out that in India there are many persons who having retired from service are not entitled to any pension or the pension to which they had made contributions do not yield adequate income in their oldage. They had drawn large amounts of money by way of gratuity, encashment of leave, provident fund etc which they had invested in a variety of interest bearing deposits and securities. Till recently, when interest rates in India were high they were getting high return on their investments. With the advent of soft interest rate regime they are at a great loss as their income from interest on the investments has fallen by more than fifty percent. In order to protect them the Government of India has had to introduce a new scheme in the budget for 2003-2004 which assures them a return of 9 per cent on their investments irrespective of the prevailing rates of interest. This is a defined benefit scheme and this is the kind of scheme that people need by way of social security.

Maintenance

Maintenance is a civil right available to give economic support to the needy persons from those who are liable to protect and maintain their spouse, children, parents, etc. In law, parents are bound to maintain minor children, major children their parents, husband his wife, and vice versa. The quantum of maintenance varies depending on the economic status of the parties. There are proposals to enhance the quanta of maintenance grants.

The right of parents without any means to be supported by their children having sufficient means has been recognized by law There is therefore nothing wrong if the elderly live with their children, contribute to the family expenses and share the shortages and surpluses joys and sorrows of the family. The current thinking therefore is to promote family values and to inculcate among the children a sense of duty to look after their elderly.

The right of parents without any means to be supported by their children has been recognized by Section 125 of the Criminal Procedure Code. The Hindu Adoptions and Maintenance Act 1956 too secures this right to parents. To simplify the procedure, provide speedy relief, lay down the machinery for processing cases and define the rights and circumstances in a comprehensive manner, the Himachal Pradesh Legislative Assembly passed the Himachal Pradesh Maintenance of Parents and Dependents Bill 1996. The Government of Maharashtra has prepared a Bill on similar lines. The National Policy on Older Persons proposes to encourage other States also to pass similar legislations so that old parents unable to maintain themselves do not face abandonment and acute neglect.

In China, on 29 August 1996, the Law of Protecting the Rights of the Elderly of the People's Republic of China was issued. This Law defines the rights of the elderly in their family life, social life and participation in social activities. The Law also provides that mainly their families should support the elderly care and that their family members should perform their duties to take care of the older persons.

All over the world, however, the joint family systems are breaking up with the result family support for the elderly is getting weakened. Besides, the principle of solidarity between the young and the old and the intergenerational relationships are also getting weakened.

The Supreme Court of India has ruled that an "aged mother has a right to be maintained by sons but that does not mean that she is entitled to live along with her sons' families. The aged mother does not have any such legal right to reside in the house of sons. Though it cannot be disputed that the sons had, before building their own houses, lived with the mother as her sons and morally were obliged to take care of her by accommodating her in their house, yet in law that obligation cannot be enlarged to a legal duty to provide her residence in the house along with their family."[13]

There are thus many contradictions in the movements for making the families responsible for the maintenance of the elderly. These contradictions will need to be harmonized.

Health

With advancing age, people develop all kinds of ailments. Higher the age the greater the susceptibility to sickness. The aged are known to be prone to various diseases, namely, degenerative changes, artioscelorisis, prostate enlargement, kidney disease, rheumatism diabetes, gout, cataract, dementia etc. The National Policy on Older Persons of the Government of India says:

> "With advancing age, old persons have to cope with health and associated problems some of which may be chronic, of a multiple nature, require constant attention and carry the risk of disability and consequent loss of autonomy. Some health problems, specially when accompanied by impaired functional capacity, require long term management of illness at home and of nursing care."

Along with the increase in life expectancy the incidence of chronic illness has also been growing. A variety of surveys carried out to assess the health status of the elderly have disclosed that more than 45 per cent of the people in the age group 60+ were suffering from chronic diseases of which joint problems were the largest with cough, blood pressure heart disease, urinary problems, piles and diabetes following in that order. Lack of adequate nutrition was one of the contributory factors for the ill health of the elderly. Studies carried out in India have found that the diet taken by the elderly was deficient in micronutrients, like iron, vitamin A, riboflavin, calcium etc. Low socio-economic status has been found to be the cause of the deficiency.

There are at present no special health care schemes for the elderly in India except the ESI and the CGHS.[14] Those who are not covered by these schemes have to depend on public dispensaries and hospitals which are notoriously inadequate or unsatisfactory in providing the services they require or they have to depend on private doctors and hospitals which are notoriously extortionist. The health insurance system has not developed fully or they do not cover the aged people above a certain age particularly if they are already suffering from disease.

National Policy for Older Persons aims at providing "good affordable health services, very heavily subsidized for the poor, and a graded system of user charges for others. It will be necessary to have a judicious mix of public health services, health insurance, health services provided by not-for-profit organizations including trusts, charities, and private medical care. While the first will require greater State participation, the second category will need to be promoted by the State, the third category given some assistance, concessions and relief and the fourth encouraged but subjected to some degree of regulation, preferably by an association of providers of private care." This policy is under implementation but its impact has not been evaluated yet.

Suggestions have been made for revamping of the primary health care system and introduction of the systems of managed care and development of health insurance in the private sector.

Long Term Care

While illness as such can be treated in a dispensary or hospital, the functional disability of old people cannot be so treated. It calls for a long term care arrangements. Advanced countries like Germany have developed schemes for long term care of the elderly. The German Dependency Insurance Act was enacted to meet the dependency care need of the elderly. Such schemes are necessary but do not exist in many countries in Asia including India.

Institutional Care

When the families of the elderly cannot look after the aged people they will have to be placed under institutional care. A variety of arrangements are possible for such care. Day care centres and oldage homes are some of them. According to Dr. Irudaya Rajan there were 728 oldage homes in India in 1998 catering to the needs of disadvantaged people including destitute persons, widows, sick people, and those with disabilities. Accomodation in one in seven oldage homes was on paying basis.

Experts have pointed out that although family care is the best form of geriatric care and institutional care should be discouraged as far as possible there is a need for more oldage homes in India. Moreover greater efforts are needed to improve the working of the homes.[15] The National Policy has recognized this need. It says: "The policy will be to consider institutional care as the last resort when personal circumstances are such that stay in oldage homes becomes absolutely necessary".

The Policy is to give assistance to voluntary organizations by way of grants in aid for construction and maintenance of oldage homes. Those for the poor will be heavily subsidized.

It is also proposed to encourage and assist voluntary organizations " to organize services such as day care, multi service citizens' centres, reach-out services, supply of disability related aids and appliances, assistance to old persons to learn to use them, short term stay services, and friendly home visits by social workers." Several voluntary organizations have come up to provide these services but their performance cannot be said to be wholly satisfactory.

Emotional Support to the Elderly

In oldage, it is not enough if one is economically secure. A person may be wealthy and may have adequate income for living in comfort but still he may feel threatened and helpless due to various reasons. Emotional insecurity may express itself in the form of loneliness, lowered life satisfaction, feeling powerless and depression. Old people need love, respect and need to feel important and wanted, more than anything else. Old people feel that the young should listen to them, ask their opinion and consult them in matters of importance. Or else they feel redundant.

Many aged people suffer more from a feeling of neglect than from any physical illness. They need company and solace. How to meet the psychological needs of the elderly is a major problem. In India there are some organizations who have specialized in catering to the whims of the elderly. And nurses are trained for the purpose. More of such organisations need to be set up.

Dr. Indira Jai Prakash, Professor of Psychology in the Bangalore University, has said that while social security assures a decent living, emotional security makes it meaningful. Social security is essential to life at any age but psychological security is necessary for the aged to enable them to enjoy the benefits that economic security bestowed. Social and emotional security together would add up to quality ageing.

According to Dr Indira Jai Prakash: "The realization that the psychological factor should be considered in promoting active ageing has come with developments in Gerontology. This field is witnessing a paradigm shift. This involves a shift of focus-from illness and disability associated with age to reserve capacity and preservation of competence:

- from frailty and dependence to positive health;
- from 'doing something for the elderly attitude to people as partners in development;
- from a curative, rehabilitative approach to successful and productive ageing;
- from treating elderly as dependants who are served by society to acknowledging that elderly can plan, manage and institute appropriate programmes for their own well being."[16]

The National Policy has also envisaged a variety of measures to promote the welfare of the aged. To what extent these measures have been implemented and their impact are yet to be evaluated.

Administration of Schemes

The social security needs of the elderly are multifaceted and they call for a unified approach but such an approach is lacking in many countries. In India for example, the problems of the elderly are dealt with by different ministries in the Central Government and State Governments with division of responsibility among the various Ministries and Departments. Take the case of the Central Government. The Ministry of Social Justice and Empowerment. deals with oldage homes; the Ministry of Rural Development deals with the National Oldage Pension Scheme; the Ministry of Labour deals with the Employees Pension Scheme, the Department of Coal deals with the Coal Mines Pension Scheme;. the Department of Pension in the Ministry of Personnel deals with pension schemes for Central Government employees; the Ministry of Health is concerned with health care of the elderly. The Ministry of Social Justice which is said to be the nodal Ministry for matters relating to the elderly evolved the National Policy for Older Persons and set up a committee to advise on the income security for the elderly without consulting the other Ministries concerned. The Central Provident Fund Commissioner, an officer of the Ministry of Labour, was appointed as a Member of the Committee and the issue became controversial. There is thus fragmentation of responsibility and lack of unity of purpose in evolving the policies concerning the elderly and in implementing them.

This situation calls for reform.

Notes and References

1. Source:UGC sponsored research project on "Sociology of Aging Among the Senior Citizens in Urban UP."
2. National Policy on Older Persons; Ministry of Social Justice and Empowerment Government of India.
3. *Ibid.*
4. *Ibid.*
5. *Ibid.*
6. ILO (1979) quoted in the *Elderly in India*, Kumudini Dandekar Sage Publications, 1996.
7. *India's Elderly*, S. Irudaya Rajan et al, Sage Publications, 1999.
8. Article 39 (e) Constitution of India.
9. Recommendation No.67 of the ILO.
10. *Social Security: A new Consensus*, ILO, Geneva, p. 62.
11. Final Report of the project OASIS Expert Committee, Ministry of Social Justice and Empowerment.
12. A time for Action by S.A.Dave, *Outlook*, March 17, 2003.
13. Anandi D Jadhav (deceased) by Lrs v Nirmala Ramachandra, Kore & Ors (2000) 2 LRI 1095 SC.
14. The Heritage Hospital is reported to have been established in Hyderabad in 1994 with complete focus on the elderly and age related issues.
15. Health status of the Elderly in India – Current Perspectives by Dr. Vinod Kumar; *Active Ageing in the New Millenium*, edited by Asbha Choudhury, Anugraha 2001.
16. Role of Intergenerational and Social Support in Active Ageing by Dr. Indira Jai Prakash; *Active Ageing in the new Millennium* edited by Aabha Choudhury, Anugraha 2001.

2

Emerging Indian Ageing Scenario

DR. S IRUDAYA RAJAN*

The ageing of population is an obvious consequence of the process of demographic transition. Being ahead, the developed regions of the world have experienced its consequences and the developing world is ready to face a similar scene. Though the proportion of elderly (defined in terms of those aged 60 and above in a population) seems to be low in some of the developing countries, they have more elderly persons in absolute terms because of their large population base. The recent emphasis on studies pertaining to the elderly in the developing world is attributed to their increasing numbers and deteriorating conditions. While their increasing number is attributed to demographic transition, their deteriorating condition is the end result of the fast eroding traditional family system in the wake of rapid modernisation, migraton and urbanisation. Projected increases in both the absolute and relative size of the elderly population in many third world countries are a subject of growing concern for social policy (Treas and Logue, 1986; Grigsby 1993; World Bank 1994). These increases are the result of changing fertility and mortality regimes over the last forty to fifty years. The combination of high fertility and falling mortality during the twentieth century has ensured that there will be large and rapid increase in elderly population as successively larger cohorts enter the span of old age. Further, the recent sharp decline in fertility is bound to lead to an increasing share of future elderly. Moreover, given that these demographic changes have been accompanied by rapid and profound socio-economic change, cohorts might differ in their experience as they become aged.

Against this backdrop, we may preface our discussion with an account of the structure and magnitude of the elderly. The number of elderly in the developing countries has been growing at a phenomenal rate; in 1990 the population of persons of 60 years and above in the developing countries exceeded that of the developed countries. Most

* Centre for Development Studies, Thiruvanathapuram, Kerala, India.

of this growth took place in developing countries and over half of it was in Asia (World Bank 1994). Obviously, the two major population giants of Asia, namely India (Irudaya Rajan, Mishra and Sarma, 1996; 1999; 2000) and China (Irudaya Rajan, 1994) naturally contributed a significant proportion of this growing elderly.

Ageing: Global Scenario

The population of the world in 1995 was 5.7 billion and it is expected to reach 10.8 billion by 2050. Between 1950 and 2150, the world population would increase fourfold. Interestingly, between 1995 and 2000, it is estimated that 81 million people would be added to the world population each year. (United Nations, 1998). The likely future (assuming medium fertility) scenario of world population will be as follows (Table 2.1).

Table 2.1: Global Scenario of Aged, 1995-2150

Year	Population (billion)	% aged 60+	% aged 65+	% aged 80+
1995	5.687	9.5	6.5	1.1
2000	6.091	9.9	6.8	1.1
2025	8.039	14.6	10.8	1.7
2050	9.367	20.7	15.1	3.4
2075	10.066	24.8	19.1	5.3
2100	10.414	27.7	22.0	7.1
2125	10.614	29.2	23.6	8.6
2150	10.806	30.5	24.9	9.8

Source: United Nations. 1998. World Population Projections to 2150. Department of Economic and Social Affairs, Population Division, United Nations, New York.

The percentage of elderly in the world population will increase rapidly from 9.5 in 1995 to 20.7 in 2050 and to 30.5 in 2150 (Table 2.1). In absolute numbers, this will mean an increase from 542 million in 1995 to 1.9 billion in 2050 and to 3.3 billion in 2150. Although in 1995, the number of children below 15 years was estimated to be 3.3 times higher than the aged 60 and above, the elderly are expected to surpass the number of children by 2050.

Among the elderly, the number of the oldest old—those aged 80 or over—will increase more rapidly over time. According to the projections, the number of those aged 80 and over will get multiplied by a factor of 17 between 1995 and 2150; from 61 million in 1995 to 320 million in 2050 and to 1054 million by 2150.

According to the assessment of the United Nations, only Western Europe in the whole world had a proportion of elderly above 15 per cent in 1950 (Table 2.2). In 2000, all the three regions of Europe

Table 2.2: Aging in Major Regions of the World, 1950-2050

Region	Percentage Aged 60 and above			
	1950	2000	2025	2050
World	8.1	9.9	14.6	20.7
More Developed	11.7	19.3	27.0	31.2
Less Developed	6.4	7.6	12.3	19.2
Least Developed	5.4	4.8	6.2	11.6
Sub-Saharan Africa	5.0	4.7	5.8	10.6
Africa	5.1	5.0	6.5	11.8
Eastern Africa	4.8	4.3	5.1	10.1
Middle Africa	5.9	4.9	5.1	9.3
Northern Africa	5.6	6.2	10.6	18.9
Southern Africa	6.0	6.6	9.7	16.0
Western Africa	4.6	4.6	5.8	10.4
Asia	6.7	8.7	14.4	21.9
Eastern Asia	7 4	11.0	19.6	26.9
South Central Asia	6.1	7.0	11.3	19.5
South Eastern Asia	5.9	7.2	12.5	21.2
Western Asia	7.1	7.1	10.7	17.0
Europe	12.1	20.1	27.3	32.8
Eastern Europe	9.7	18.7	24.4	31.2
Northern Europe	14.9	20.3	27.0	29.0
Southern Europe	11.3	21.5	30.1	37.2
Western Europe	15.0	21.3	29.7	34.2
Latin America and *the Caribbean*	6.0	8.0	14.1	22.2
Caribbean	6.9	9.9	15.9	21.6
Central America	6.5	6.7	12.2	21.3
South America	5.7	8.3	14.7	22.7
North America	12.4	16.4	25.0	27.4
Oceania	11.2	13.2	18.9	23.8
Australia-New Zealand	12.6	15.8	23.2	27.7
Melanesia	5.8	5.4	8.2	15.4
Micronesia	3.1	5.0	9.4	16.5
Polynesia	4.0	7.0	11.9	21.7

Source: United Nations. 1998. World Population Prospects. The 1996 Revision. Department of Economic and Social Affairs, United Nations, New York.

except Eastern Europe registered a proportion above 20. In other words, one-fifth of the European population is elderly. In the next 50 years, the proportion of the aged is expected to grow more rapidly. As of today, Southern Europe has the highest proportion of elderly (21.5%) and it is expected to reach 37.2 percent by 2050. In the developing countries, one in every twelve is now elderly and it is expected to become one in five by 2050. In the developed countries, the ratio is already one in five now and it is projected to reach one in three by 2050.

Ageing: Asian Scenario

Though Asia as a whole accounts for only 9 per cent of elderly, there are variations between the various regions (Table 3). While Eastern Asia leads with 11 percent as of 2000 the corresponding proportion for other regions is only 7 percent. By the year 2050, one in four in Eastern Asia, one in five in South Central and Eastern Asia and one in six in Western Asia are expected to be elderly. Out of 36 countries under study, not a single country had a proportion of elderly above 10 percent in 1950. Presently, seven countries in Asia have crossed 10 percent and one country (Japan) in Eastern Asia, the proportion is already 23 (for more details on Japan's elderly and social policy, see Bass, Morris and Oka, 1996).

Table 2.3: Ageing in Asia, 1950-2050

Country	Percentage Aged 60 and above			
	1950	2000	2025	2050
Asia	6.7	8.7	14.4	21.9
Eastern Asia	7.4	11.0	19.6	26.9
China	7.5	10.0	18.5	26.2
Hong Kong	3.7	15.0	32.4	38.9
Japan	7.7	22.6	32.1	36.0
Mongolia	5.5	5.6	10.0	20.2
Republic of Korea	5.4	10.5	21.8	28.8
South Central Asia	6.1	7.0	11.3	19.5
Afghanistan	3.4	4.6	6.1	9.9
Bangladesh	6.2	5.2	9.0	19.9
Bhutan	5.8	5.2	6.3	10.6
India	5.6	7.6	12.6	21.3
Iran	8.3	5.8	8.0	16.5
Maldives	8.2	5.0	5.9	12.1

Nepal	7.1	5.4	7.1	13.5
Pakistan	8.2	4.9	8.2	15.1
Sri Lanka	6.0	9.6	17.0	25.2
South Eastern Asia	5.9	7.2	12.5	21.2
Cambodia	4.5	4.8	8.7	14.6
Indonesia	6.2	7.4	12.7	21.6
Lao	4.6	4.8	6.0	11.0
Malaysia	7.3	6.5	12.5	21.1
Myammar	5.5	7.0	10.8	18.8
Philippines	5.5	5.7	10.9	18.7
Singapore	3.7	10.4	27.8	29.1
Thailand	4.8	8.7	17.9	28.1
Vietnam	6.5	7.3	11.9	22.1
West Asia	7.1	7.1	10.7	17.0
Bahrain	4.6	4.9	19.6	24.3
Cyprus	9.1	15.3	22.3	26.1
Iraq	4.3	4.9	7.5	14.7
Israel	6.3	12.7	18.1	24.4
Jordan	7.4	4.6	6.6	13.4
Kuwait	4.5	3.6	16.0	24.7
Oman	5.0	3.9	5.5	8.4
Qatar	5.7	4.8	24.1	19.8
Saudi Arabia	5.6	4.6	8.8	13.3
Syria	6.8	4.7	7.7	18.1
Turkey	5.9	8.7	14.7	23.9
Emirates	5.7	5.0	22.7	23.4
Yemen	6.2	3.7	4.3	8.8

Source: United Nations, 1998, World Population Prospects. The 1996 Revision, Department of Economic and Social Affairs, United Nations, New York.

By 2050, the proportion of elderly in all the thirty three countries in Asia except Afghanistan, Oman and Yemen are projected to be above 10 per cent. Among them, in 10 countries the proportions are likely to cross 20 per cent, 6 countries having 25 per cent elderly and 2 countries as large as 35 per cent. Hong Kong is predicted to lead with 39 percent of elderly, followed by Japan. Two populous countries in the world (China and India) will share the major proportion of world's elderly. Currently, one in ten Chinese is an elderly and this ratio is expected to reach one in 4 by 2050. Similarly, one in 12 Indians is an elderly and this ratio is likely to be one in 5 in 2050. In absolute terms, India's elderly population is expected to increase from 76 million in 2000 to 327 million in 2050 and that of China from 127 million to 397 million during the same period (United Nations, 1998).

Ageing: Indian Scenario

According to the 1991 census, India consisting of 25 states and 7 Union Territories had an elderly population of 56 million. Among the Indian states, Uttar Pradesh led the rest with 9 million elderly, followed by Maharashtra (5.5 million), Bihar (5.2 million) and Madhya Pradesh (4.3 million). The lowest elderly population was enumerated in Lakshadweep. With regard to the composition of the elderly, the old-old (70+) numbered 20 million, the states of Uttar Pradesh and Maharashtra having a major share of them. The same situation was observed across states and Union territories (see Table 2.4).

The proportion of elderly persons in India has risen from 5.63 per cent in 1961 to 6.58 in 1991 (Irudaya Rajan, Mishra and Sarma, 1999). Given the differences in mortality and fertility transition across Indian states and union territories the highest proportion of elderly is found in Kerala (8.77 per cent) and the lowest (3.55 per cent) is reported in Andaman and Nicobar Islands. The All India proportion of old-old was 2.4 per cent in 1991. As expected, Kerala also has the highest proportion old-old with 3.46 (for details, see Irudaya Rajan, Mishra and Ramanathan, 1993; Zachariah and Irudaya Rajan, 1997; Mari Bhat and Irudaya Rajan, 1990; Guilmoto and Irudaya Rajan, 1998).

India is one of the few countries in the world where males outnumber females. This phenomenon among elderly is of prime importance as female life expectancy at ages 60 and 70 are slightly higher than that of males. However, at any given age, there are more widows than widowers. Reasons for this unusual phenomenon need to be identified in the wider context. For instance, since the beginning of the 20th century, life expectancy at birth among Indian males had been higher than females until the first half of the 1990s. Besides this unusual demographic pattern of excess female mortality at infant and childhood ages, the analysis is further hampered by the phenomenon of age exaggeration among the aged. Thus, the above findings of more males in old age does not reveal a true picture of situation among elderly persons (for details, see Mari Bhat, 1992).

Table 2.4: Demographic Profile of the Aged, 1991 Census

States	Population (000's)		Percentage to total population		Sex ratio (f/m)*100	
	(60+)	(70+)	(60+)	(70+)	(60+)	(70+)
Andhra Pradesh	4306	1425	6.47	2.14	102	106
Arunachal Pradesh	37	12	4.23	1.42	83	90
Assam	1186	448	5.29	2.00	81	76
Bihar	5227	1803	6.05	2.09	86	85
Goa	74	27	6.34	2.27	131	141
Gujarat	2540	966	6.15	2.34	107	113
Haryana	1230	528	7.47	3.21	93	81
Himachal Pradesh	402	164	7.79	3.18	89	87
Jammu & Kashmir	432	163	5.78	2.18	77	75
Karnataka	3041	1149	6.76	2.56	101	105
Kerala	2549	1006	8.77	3.46	115	121
Madhya Pradesh	4254	1583	6.43	2.39	98	100
Maharashtra	5453	1934	6.91	2.45	101	105
Manipur	109	40	5.94	2.19	88	92
Meghalaya	82	29	4.62	1.64	83	86
Mizoram	34	12	4.93	1.77	96	105
Nagaland	65	28	5.40	2.31	71	69
Orissa	2217	794	6.98	2.51	99	98
Punjab	1532	625	7.56	3.08	83	78
Rajasthan	2666	917	6.06	2.08	98	103
Sikkim	19	6	4.59	1.51	75	78
Tamil Nadu	4073	1408	7.29	2.52	92	90
Tripura	192	87	6.96	3.17	97	100
Uttar Pradesh	9250	3403	6.65	2.45	81	77
West Bengal	4087	1500	6.00	2.20	96	96
Andaman & Nichobar	10	3	3.55	1.18	67	78
Chandigarh	29	11	4.52	1.73	83	87
Dadra Nagar Haveli	6	2	4.40	1.24	122	140
Daman & Diu	6	2	6.32	2.43	150	168
Delhi	444	154	4.71	1.63	85	86
Lakshadweep	3	1	5.22	1.68	92	93
Pondicherry	56	21	6.90	2.55	108	105
All India	55606	20252	6.58	2.40	94	93

Source: Irudaya Rajan, Mishra and Sarma, 2000

In the Indian situation, the sex ratio (females per 100 males) of the aged as well as the old-old persons (beyond the age of 70), favours males. Only 9 states and union territories reported a sex ratio above 100 indicating excess of females over males in old age. Reasons for more males in old age may consist of under-reporting of females, specially widows, age exaggeration, low female life expectancy at birth and excess female mortality among infants, children and adults besides historical factors. Not withstanding the several analytical and statistical problems, it cannot be disputed that the preponderance of females in extreme old ages need to be brought to the attention of planners and policy makers (for more details, see Sudha and Irudaya Rajan, 1999; Mari Bhat, Navaneetham and S Irudaya Rajan, 1995).

According to the 1991 census, seventy eight percent of the Indian elderly lived in rural areas. The percentage of aged in rural areas was 7.22 compared to 5.37 in urban areas. Detailed analysis indicates that states and territories have shown similar type of rural-urban proportion indicating more elderly with a rural residential background. Over the last 20 years, the rural share of elderly has been increasing steadily; out of 100 elderly persons in India, four-fifths are found in rural areas. (Irudaya Rajan, Mishra, Sarma, 1999).

Available research on ageing suggests that fertility plays a predominant role in inducing the ageing process compared to mortality. As far as India is concerned, there has been a substantial reduction in mortality compared to fertility since 1950. For instance, while the crude birth rate for India declined from 47.3 during 1951-61 to 22.8 in 1996, the crude death rate fell steeply from 28.5 to 8.4 during the same period. Logically, therefore, India is expected to have a faster decline in fertility in the immediate future compared to mortality because mortality is already at a low level. The ageing process in India will, therefore, be faster than in other developing countries. Moreover, transition from high to low fertility is expected to narrow the age structure at its base and broaden the same at the top. In addition, improvement in life expectancy at all ages will allow more old people to survive thus intensifying the ageing process. In this context, an examination of the increasing life expectancy indicates that the gain is going to be shared more and more by older people which will make them live still longer (Irudaya Rajan and Mishra, 1995).

The broad age structure in any population reflects the changing composition of children (0-14), adults of working ages (15-59) and the elderly persons (60+). The proportion of children has declined by

3.4 units between 1961-91. The 3.4 units' decline among children was shared between adults (2.4 points) and elderly (1.0 point) respectively.

Table 2.5: Measures of Population Aging, 1991 Census

	Dependency Ratios			Median	Index	Proportion
	Young	Old	Total	Age	of Aging	(60+)
Andhra Pradesh	61.8	11.2	73.1	22.6	18.1	6.5
Arunachal Pradesh	71.0	7.6	78.6	20.6	10.7	4.2
Assam	69.7	9.5	79.2	20.4	13.6	5.3
Bihar	78.0	11.5	89.5	19.9	14.7	6.1
Goa	56.8	10.7	68.5	22.6	18.5	6.3
Gujarat	64.5	10.8	75.3	21.7	16.7	6.2
Haryana	76.7	14.3	91.0	19.8	18.6	7.5
Himachal Pradesh	67.4	14.1	81.5	21.2	21.0	7.8
Jammu & Kashmir	62.2	10.0	72.1	21.1	16.0	5.8
Karnataka	62.6	11.8	74.4	22.2	18.8	6.8
Kerala	49.9	14.4	64.3	24.4	28.9	8.8
Madhya Pradesh	73.7	11.9	85.6	20.6	16.2	6.4
Maharashtra	60.7	11.9	72.7	22.9	19.6	6.9
Manipur	62.8	10.3	73.1	21.5	16.4	5.9
Meghalaya	68.8	8.2	77.0	20.3	11.9	4.6
Mizoram	63.7	8.5	72.2	20.8	13.3	4.9
Nagaland	60.3	9.1	69.4	21.1	15.2	5.4
Orissa	64.4	12.3	76.7	22.2	19.2	7.0
Punjab	62.7	13.3	76.0	22.1	21.2	7.6
Rajasthan	76.7	11.4	88.1	19.8	14.9	6.1
Sikkim	67.5	8.1	75.6	20.1	11.9	4.6
Tamil Nadu	51.4	11.9	63.3	24.5	23.2	7.3
Tripura	66.0	12.4	78.4	21.6	18.8	6.9
Uttar Pradesh	76.8	12.6	89.4	19.9	16.4	6.7
West Bengal	62.5	10.4	72.9	22.2	16.6	6.0
Andaman & Nicobar	53.5	5.7	59.2	22.6	10.6	3.6
Chandigarh	44.9	6.9	51.8	24.6	15.3	4.5
Dadra & Nagar Haveli	61.7	7.5	69.2	21.7	12.1	4.4
Daman & Diu	55.6	10.5	66.1	22.1	18.9	6.3
Delhi	54.2	7.6	61.8	23.0	14.1	4.7
Lakshadweep	64.0	9.0	73.0	21.3	14.1	5.2
Pondicherry	57.4	11.7	69.1	22.8	20.3	6.9
All India	67.0	11.8	78.7	21.6	17.6	6.6

Source: Irudaya Rajan, Mishra and Sarma, 1999.

Median age is defined as the point which divides the population into two equal halves and which reflects the ageing phenomenon. It increases faster with the fertility decline which reduces the number of children. For India, it is computed as 20 years for 1981 and 22 years in 1991. Among the states and union territories, this index varies substantially with 3 states and union territories having almost 25 years, another four states having less than 20 years and the rest being between 20 to 25 years as of 1991.

Index of ageing is defined as the ratio of population above 60 years of age to children in ages, 0-14. It is interpreted as the number of children below the age of 14 years per hundred persons above the age of 60. On the basis of this index, the ageing process was much slower in India during 1961-91 and is expected to increase sharply in the future. States and union territories such as Goa, Kerala, Tamil Nadu and Chandigarh, which are ahead in the demographic transition, have shown a higher index value. Though the proportion of aged for the country was only around 7 percent in 1991, still it has the highest number of elderly persons in South Central Asia (See Table 2.5). Moreover, ageing process is intensified owing to higher survival of elderly persons beyond ages 60 and 70. Table 2.6 provides evidence to this effect in India. As can be seen, males are expected to live 17 years beyond age 60 and 10 years beyond age 70 and the corresponding years for females are 18 and 11 respectively by 2021. (Irudaya Rajan and Mishra, 1995).

Table 2.6: Expectation of life at ages 60 and 70 for India.

Year	Male		Female	
	60	70	60	70
1971	13.80	8.57	14.75	9.10
1981	14.25	8.83	15.31	9.42
1991	15.01	9.27	16.23	9.97
2001	15.74	9.70	17.05	10.45
2011	16.29	10.03	17.75	10.87
2021	16.75	10.32	18.18	11.14

Source: Estimated by the authors.

Dependency Ratios refer to the ratio of the population below 14 years of age and above 60 years of age to the population in working ages (15-59). This also exhibits the changing age structure of population in relation to young and old dependency. Both young and total dependency ratios have shown a consistent decline over a period up time whereas the old dependency ratios exhibit an increase. The old dependency ratio was 11.8 for the 1991 census and the young dependency ratio was 67.0. In understanding dependency among the old, it is assumed that all those beyond the age of sixty years are dependent. But the available data indicates that many of the elderly are self-dependent or still working and therefore can not be treated as dependent. Old age dependency estimated on the basis of non-workers shows a much lower value than the one estimated on the basis of age only. Such an exercise in the case of India for 1991 brings down the ratio from 11.8 to 7.42. Further, the non-workers in Indian census include rentier/pensioners, beggars and those in household duties who may otherwise be considered economically productive and hence exclusion of these category of non-workers further reduces the old age dependency to 4.56 (for more details, see Irudaya Rajan, Mishra and Sarma, 1999).

Emerging Ageing Scenario, 2001-2051

One of the major objectives of this paper is to assess the emerging ageing scenario of India in the first half of 21st century (2001-2051). Towards this end, we have projected the elderly population of 25 states and 7 union territories by dividing the country into six major regions: south, west, central, east, north and northeast (see Table 2.7). Table 2.7 gives the distribution of the elderly falling in the 60+ category and Tables 2.8 and 2.9 that of those falling in the 70+ and 80+ category. All three tables profile the region-wise elderly classified by ages 60 and above, 70 and above and 80 and above in terms of size, proportion and gender. The emerging age structure of India is presented by the age pyramids.

Table 2.7: Number, Proportion and Sex Ratio of Elderly (60+), 2001-2051

	Absolute Numbers (millions)					
Region	2001	2011	2021	2031	2041	2051
South	18.60	25.49	34.64	46.28	59.32	69.73
West	10.59	14.66	20.60	27.56	35.29	43.66
Central	16.17	21.03	28.13	37.09	50.86	69.88
East	15.03	20.86	29.36	38.77	51.39	67.33
North	8.23	11.17	15.92	22.17	30.04	39.01
Northeast	2.16	3.09	4.67	6.72	9.10	11.35
India	70.78	96.30	133.32	178.59	236.01	300.96

Region	Proportion 2001	2011	2021	2031	2041	2051
South	8.3	10.2	13.0	16.8	21.4	25.8
West	7.5	9.1	11.5	14.4	17.7	21.7
Central	6.4	6.8	7.5	8.4	9.9	11.9
East	6.8	8.0	9.9	11.7	14.4	17.8
North	6.6	7.4	9.0	11.1	13.6	16.5
Northeast	5.6	6.8	9.0	11.6	14.5	17.2
India	7.1	8.2	9.9	11.9	14.5	17.3

Region	Sex Ratio (m/f*1000) 2001	2011	2021	2031	2041	2051
South	954	966	942	897	927	939
West	980	1005	1000	974	1005	985
Central	1114	1069	1020	995	1084	1072
East	1070	1074	1030	975	1014	1018
North	1067	1070	1048	1025	1063	1028
Northeast	1139	1139	1084	985	978	993
India	1036	1034	1004	964	1008	1007

Note: According to the 1991 census, India was administratively divided into 25 states and 7 Union Territories. To make the discussion more meaningful, we have classified the 32 units into 6 regions geographically. Population Projections are made by the author.

South: Andhra Pradesh, Kerala, Karnataka, Tamil Nadu, Pondicherry and Lakshadweep (6)

West: Goa, Gujarat, Maharashtra, Daman and Diu and Dadra Nagar Haveli (5)

Central: Madhya Pradesh and Uttar Pradesh (2)

East: Bihar, Orissa, West Bengal and Andaman & Nicobar Islands (4);

North: Delhi, Haryana, Himachal Pradesh, Jammu & Kashmir, Punjab, Rajasthan and Chandigarh (7);

North East: Arunachal Pradesh, Assam, Manipur, Meghalaya, Mizoram, Nagaland, Tripura and Sikkim (8)

A few comments on the projections are called for. We have used the 1991 census age structure as the base population and the assumptions on fertility and mortality are based on the past trends as revealed from the Sample Registration System in India. The projection period is 1991 to 2051; the number of projected elderly persons in 2051 are already born in 1991. Given our assumptions regarding mortality, the projections are likely to be valid.

India's elderly population aged 60 and above is expected to increase from 71 million in 2001 to 179 million in 2031 and further to 301 million in 2051. The proportion is likely to reach 12 in 2031 and 17 in 2051. As of 2001, South India has the highest number of elderly persons above 60 years and maintain its lead in the next 40 years (19 million in 2001 to 70 million in 2051). In fact, one-fourth of India's elderly persons live in South India indicating the low fertility and high expectation of life at birth in the region (Guilmoto and Irudaya Rajan, 1998; Irudaya Rajan and Zachariah, 1998) The lowest numbers are expected in Northeast India. In fact, Central India with the second highest number of elderly in 2001 is projected to increase its population at the same phase as South India at 2051. East India also follows South and Central India and is expected to reach 67 million in 2051. No region in India had in 2001 a proportion of elderly population above 10 per cent.

Only South India is projected to reach 10 percent in 2011 while West India is expected to have an elderly population above 10 per cent in 2021. However, except Central India, all other regions of India are projected to reach above 10 percent in 2031. Around 2051, South India is expected to have an elderly population above 25 per cent, followed by West India with above 20 per cent and another three regions (East, North and Northeast) are with above 15 per cent and the lowest is expected in Central India. Excess elderly females are noted only in South India throughout the period under study. As long as other regions of India have excess males in the ages 60 and above, it is interesting to examine the reasons for excess eldery males which is contrary to the other developing nations.

The number of elderly persons above 70 years of age (old-old) is likely to increase sharper than 60 years and above. The old-old is projected to increase around 5 times between 2001 to 2051 (27 million in 2001 to 132 million in 2051). Their proportion is expected to rise from 2.7 in 2001 to 7.6 in 2051. Another feature among the old-old is worth writing home. Though we have found excess males in the group aged 60 and above, the old-old sex ratio is very much favourable to females. In 2051, South India is expected to lead with the highest number (34 million) of old-old, followed by East and Central India and the lowest is expected in Northeast. However, the proportion of old-old is expected to be highest in South India, followed by West India and the lowest is in Central India. South and West India are projected to have excess females throughout the study periods: other regions show excess females only in some periods.

Table 2.8: Number, Proportion and Sex Ratio of Elderly (70+), 1991-2051

Region	2001	2011	2021	2031	2041	2051
	Absolute Numbers (millions)					
South	7.17	9.76	13.69	19.05	25.96	33.61
West	4.06	5.50	7.83	11.29	15.23	19.72
Central	6.15	7.78	10.54	14.56	19.53	27.84
East	5.61	7.64	10.95	15.92	21.04	28.79
North	3.29	4.15	5.93	8.77	12.44	17.20
Northeast	0.79	1.07	1.61	2.54	3.70	5.15
India	27.07	35.90	50.55	73.13	97.90	132.31
	Proportion					
	2001	2011	2021	2031	2041	2051
South	3.2	3.9	5.2	6.9	9.4	12.4
West	2.9	3.4	4.4	5.9	7.7	9.8
Central	2.5	2.5	2.8	3.3	3.8	4.8
East	2.5	2.9	3.7	4.8	5.9	7.6
North	2.6	2.8	3.4	4.4	5.7	7.3
Northeast	2.1	2.4	3.1	4.4	5.9	7.8
India	2.7	3.1	3.8	4.8	6.0	7.6
	Sex Ratio (m/f*1000)					
	2001	2011	2021	2031	2041	2051
South	897	878	902	868	818	861
West	894	922	948	927	895	937
Central	1098	1047	999	950	933	1046
East	1011	1010	1012	953	896	962
North	1007	996	1004	974	960	1011
Northeast	1091	1060	1082	1026	932	958
India	981	966	970	930	891	954

Note: Ibid.

The oldest old (80+) in India is expected to grow faster than any other age group in the population. In absolute numbers, it is likely to increase six-fold from 5.4 million in 2001 to 32.0 million in 2051. As expected, South India will lead with the highest number as well as the proportion of oldest-old in the next half of the twenty-first century. From 2011 onwards, all regions are expected to have excess oldest-old females.

Table 2.9: Number, Proportion and Sex Ratio of Elderly (80+), 1991-2051

Region	2001	2011	2021	2031	2041	2051
	Absolute Numbers (millions)					
South	1.42	2.19	3.03	4.38	6.28	8.77
West	0.81	1.21	1.68	2.47	3.67	4.99
Central	1.21	1.68	2.21	3.09	4.42	6.02
East	1.08	1.64	2.28	3.39	5.98	6.73
North	0.70	0.95	1.24	1.87	2.90	4.22
Northeast	0.15	0.21	0.31	0.49	0.82	1.25
India	5.37	7.88	10.75	15.69	23.17	31.98
	Proportion					
Region	2001	2011	2021	2031	2041	2051
South	0.6	0.9	1.1	1.6	2.3	3.2
West	0.6	0.6	0.9	1.3	1.8	2.5
Central	0.5	0.5	0.6	0.7	0.9	1.0
East	0.5	0.6	0.8	1.0	1.4	1.8
North	0.6	0.6	0.7	0.9	1.3	1.8
Northeast	0.4	0.5	0.6	0.9	1.3	1.9
India	0.5	0.7	0.8	1.0	1.4	1.8
	Sex Ratio (m/f*1000)					
Region	2001	2011	2021	2031	2041	2051
South	859	781	760	765	700	644
West	848	803	819	812	752	713
Central	1199	1040	980	898	820	797
East	1067	928	919	878	785	724
North	1052	894	893	882	838	826
Northeast	1104	986	991	1021	967	904
India	998	884	866	843	774	732

Note: Ibid.

The old age dependency ratio for India and the different regions within the country are almost similar in 1991 except Northeast India. However, the trend is expected to be different in 2051; 100 persons in the age group 15-59 will have to support 42 persons above 60 and more in South India (Table 2.10). The ratios are 35 for West India and 28 for India as a whole. As of 2001, India has 20 elderly per 100 children and the index is expected to reach 80 in 2051. South India and West India are expected to have more elderly persons above 60 and above compared to children. The projected indices are 172 and 127 respectively.

Table 2.10: Indices of Ageing, 1991-2051

Region	2001	2011	2021	2031	2041	2051
			Old Dependency Ratio			
South	13.2	15.9	19.8	25.8	34.1	42.3
West	12.3	14.4	18.1	22.4	28.0	34.9
Central	11.6	11.9	12.9	13.9	16.2	19.6
East	11.5	13.1	15.8	18.5	22.7	28.7
North	11.2	12.3	14.7	17.8	21.9	26.7
Northeast	9.5	11.1	14.3	18.4	23.3	27.6
India	11.9	13.4	16.0	19.0	23.2	28.2
			Index of Ageing			
	2001	2011	2021	2031	2041	2051
South	29.1	40.3	60.0	88.6	126.5	171.5
West	24.2	32.6	46.0	65.7	90.6	126.6
Central	17.0	19.0	22.3	27.1	34.6	46.1
East	20.1	25.9	35.0	46.7	63.7	87.5
North	18.7	22.8	30.7	42.1	57.1	76.5
Northeast	16.3	21.7	32.3	45.8	63.0	82.4
India	2 1.1	26.5	35.2	46.8	62.0	81.7

Note: Ibid.

Social and Economic Characteristic

Besides demographic assessment, it is also pertinent to understand some characteristics of elderly such as the level of literacy, marital status and work status as revealed from the Indian censuses. These analyses will enlighten the policy makers regarding the needs of the elderly and the remedial measures that can be adopted for making the old persons real assets rather than being considered as liabilities in the present day society. Literacy, a prominent social indicator, will reflect the extent to which the older people can be made conscious of their rights. Further their marital status will provide an insight into their way of life. Lastly the nature of their economic dependence can be viewed from their employment status. Any policy regarding the elderly should thus take note of their literacy levels, and marital and work status.

Literacy

The well being of the elderly is intimately linked with their past educational record as education enables smoother adaptability to changing socio-economic conditions. A literate according to the Indian census is defined as a person having the ability to read and write with an understanding in any regional language.

The data shows the dismally low level of literacy among the aged. There remains a greater degree of discrepancy between the level of literacy in the general population and the aged. A low level of literacy among the older population is understandable as they have spent much of their lives prior to the advent of the period of accelerated socio-economic development in the country. With a low overall literacy level in the country, the differential between younger and older generations is yet to narrow down. The rural elderly seem to be more disadvantaged in this respect as both quantity and quality of educational facilities in rural areas have been quite inferior to those existing in urban areas in the past. Older women are the least literate because of the existing gender differentials in literacy levels in the general population. Higher educational levels are most uncommon among the elderly. Though the current literacy level among the aged is pretty low, the future elderly are expected to be more literate and hence more demanding in terms of their rights and privileges. Is the government of India ready to restructure the expenditure pattern to suit the needs of the elderly in the future?

The literacy rate among elderly females in 1991 was 12.68 per cent - 30.76 per cent and 7.51 per cent in urban and rural areas respectively (Table 2.11). In other words, out of 100 elderly rural women, there were only 8 literates! The trend between 1961 and 1991 censuses reveal the following points; literacy levels among elderly persons are low. It is extremely low in rural areas and especially so among women. In 1961, only one state (Kerala) in India had a rural female literacy of 15 per cent and many states and union territories had literacy levels below 5 pe rcent. The situation has however changed considerably after 30 years as shown by the 1991 census. As of 1991, six states and union territories had elderly female literacy levels above

25 percent and only two states (Arunachal Pradesh and Rajasthan) had a literacy rate below 5 percent. It is noteworthy that half of the female elderly in Kerala are literate.

Table 2.11: Literacy Rate Among the Aged, 1961-1991

State	Male			Female		
	1961	1981	1991	1961	1981	1991
Andhra Pradesh	22.66	28.21	30.88	3.39	6.15	8.78
Arunchal Pradesh	n.a	5.58	11.32	n.a	1.05	2.62
Assam	30.05	n.a	43.27	7.89	n.a	11.70
Bihar	26.56	29.08	32.12	2.20	3.89	5.85
Goa	40.23	53.65	60.49	13.56	20.52	26.02
Gujarat	35.88	41.63	44.91	5.93	11.78	12.65
Haryana	n.a	23.08	27.46	n.a	3.76	5.80
Himachal Pradesh	15.01	23.08	29.99	1.05	3.76	5.01
Jammu & Kashmir	n.a	17.05	n.a	n.a	1.81	n.a
Karnataka	30.78	39.77	44.91	4.01	8.39	12.65
Kerala	52.70	66.07	78.20	16.04	32.85	52.30
Madhya Pradesh	22.69	26.56	32.18	1.93	3.64	6.33
Maharashtra	31.01	42.69	48.61	4.54	9.07	13.88
Manipur	28.22	26.27	37.85	1.43	2.06	7.13
Meghalaya	n.a	30.43	34.21	n.a	12.39	16.68
Mizoram	n.a	65.05	77.06	n.a	23.32	42.62
Nagaland	6.13	15.83	30.50	1.53	4.76	12.84
Orissa	36.29	44.40	47.71	2.24	4.72	8.06
Punjab	22.50	23.94	29.43	2.94	4.55	7.83
Rajasthan	19.21	21.71	24.81	1.78	2.75	4.18
Sikkim	20.51	28.42	29.73	1.43	2.48	5.10
Tamil Nadu	40.37	47.88	49.94	5.71	10.88	16.07
Tripura	33.58	47.27	50.55	3.55	10.63	15.31
Uttar Pradesh	21.26	24.01	30.72	2.43	3.45	6.15
West Bengal	45.68	51.78	59.59	9.35	12.81	20.33
Andaman and Nicobar Islands	35.76	42.50	50.62	6.35	9.93	16.13
Chandigarh	n.a	66.37	72.90	n.a	32.77	42.56
Dadar & Nagar Haveli	10.20	16.73	19.93	1.21	3.85	5.48
Daman & Diu	n.a	n.a	61.96	n.a	n.a	14.25
Delhi	54.01	62.60	68.99	18.75	27.55	36.71
Lakshadweep	25.17 5	4.35	62.49	2.57	5.99	16.16
Pondicherry	51.71	57.90	60.77	11.03	18.16	25.39
All India	**29.18**	**34.79**	**40.62**	**4.30**	**7.89**	**12.68**

Surprisingly, between 1961 and 1991, the literacy levels among rural elderly women trebled not only in India in general but also in most of the states and union territories. Still the levels are pretty low among rural women. The planners and policy makers should take note of the increasing literacy levels among elderly because the future elderly are expected to demand more social, financial and health services compared to the present generation of old persons.

Marital Status

Marital status of the elderly gains prominence from the consensus that married ones fare batter than the single ones on a number of dimensions, e.g., economic, social, emotional and care giving at older ages (Myers 1986). A major concern is the increasing proportion of women in general and those widowed in particular. A much lower proportion of men is widowed compared to women in extreme old ages. Two prominent reasons cited for this extent of gender disparity in widowhood consist of (i) the longer life of women compared to men and (ii) the universal tendency for women to marry men older than themselves. Also widowed men are much more likely to remarry and thus overcome their widowed status. Though the relationship between elderly wellbeing and their marital status cannot be spelt out precisely, any change in the marital status composition of the elderly deserves special attention.

Currently married males accounted for 80.7 percent in 1991 census against 44.2 per cent for females. On the other hand, 54.0 percent of elderly women were widows as against 15.5 per cent widowers. However, it has been shown that the gap in the widowhood proportion gets narrowed down among the old-old (70+). More than 67 per cent of women aged 70 and above were widows in India as of 1991. For the first time, the 1991 census provided the martial status by age up to 80 Plus after the recommendation made by us in an earlier study (Irudaya Rajan, Mishra and Sarma, 1996). The results are presented in detail for all major states and union territories, as we felt, widowhood is an handicap in old age and they deserve social safety nets irrespective of sex. Striking differences are observed between widows and widowers. At age 80, one in four male elderly is a widower whereas three in four female elderly are widows (see Table 2.12).

Table 2.12: Percentage of Widowers and Widows among 60 Plus, 70 Plus and 80 Plus, 1991

	Widowers			Widows		
States	60+	70+	80+	60+	70+	80+
Andhra Pradesh	12.7	17.7	22.5	63.1	76.8	80.7
Arunchal Pradesh	9.1	16.2	19.0	49.1	55.3	58.7
Assam	12.3	15.9	20.2	55.7	66.3	70.4
Bihar	15.9	20.7	22.0	45.4	56.2	55.7
Goa	13.1	19.7	28.5	65.9	75.3	79.8
Gujarat	15.7	22.4	25.8	52.7	66.8	69.7
Haryana	17.2	24.0	33.9	36.5	55.9	69.4
Himachal Pradesh	16.8	23.9	32.1	56.0	71.2	80.9
Karnataka	12.5	18.0	23.0	63.2	75.3	77.9
Kerala	12.9	14.3	22.4	58.0	60.5	77.5
Madhya Pradesh	17.2	23.0	24.1	54.0	67.1	67.9
Maharashtra	16.7	23.7	25.4	59.5	72.8	77.9
Manipur	10.9	15.9	21.9	40.9	54.2	62.0
Meghalaya	10.5	14.9	19.2	43.7	53.9	58.8
Mizoram	16.5	24.6	29.4	38.7	54.7	65.4
Nagaland	7.2	10.1	12.0	24.5	31.5	37.3
Orissa	18.1	26.1	28.9	39.5	55.4	75.6
Punjab	17.5	25.3	35.7	55.5	72.1	85.1
Rajasthan	38.0	24.5	33.7	36.8	45.8	81.4
Sikkim	14.9	21.6	24.6	32.1	42.8	47.8
Tamil Nadu	20.5	26.6	25.7	42.8	55.0	75.9
Tripura	11.4	15.6	20.8	60.4	71.9	79.6
Uttar Pradesh	11.0	14.9	28.6	65.1	75.3	54.6
West Bengal	12.3	15.9	15.8	55.7	66.3	72.1
Andaman and Nicobar	9.1	11.9	13.8	49.1	61.0	61.0
Chandigarh	10.3	16.9	23.7	35.2	48.3	55.6
Dadar & Nagar Haveli	14.1	21.1	24.9	55.1	67.0	77.2
Daman & Diu	13.7	21.6	33.9	66.6	80.0	89.3
Delhi	14.0	22.0	31.2	44.6	60.5	69.1
Lakshadweep	10.7	19.2	21.4	60.3	72.7	75.0
Pondicherry	15.4	21.4	29.3	67.7	80.4	85.1
All India	**15.5**	**21.4**	**25.4**	**54.0**	**67.2**	**69.8**

Work Status

Some studies have attempted to explain the consequences of the ageing phenomenon on the basis of the conventional dependency ratios. A more satisfactory approach in this respect however is to base our conclusions on the basis of field surveys on work status according to assets including land etc. Sample surveys conducted in rural India in general reflects a greater degree of financial insecurity among the aged. Inadequate financial resources has been indicated as one of the major problem of the Indian elderly (Desai, 1985). The financial inadequacy seems to be of a higher degree among female elderly compared to their male counterparts (Dak and Sharma 1987; Nandal, Khatri and Kadian, 1987).

Another significant finding was with regard to losing economic independence with the increase in age (Kaur, Grover and Aggarwal, 1987). In many situations, it has also been found that rural elderly continue to work though their number of working hours comes down with increasing age (Singh, Singh and Sharma, 1987). While examining economic sufficiency in another context, the same authors established that financial problems are more common among widows and among elderly in nuclear families. They also indicated that economic insecurity is related to class and caste. Another observation in this regard by Punia and Sharma (1987) finds economic insecurity to be the sole concern of elderly in barely sustainable households in rural India. The major sources of worries of the elderly consist of social strain and the economic dependence. The worries on social relation is more compared to economic worries for those who live in nuclear families or living alone (Shah 1993). These worries are in terms of what will happen to them in case of sickness or disability. On the other hand financial worries have their bearing on the social class they belong to.

According to the National Sample Survey (1986-87) 34.02 percent of the rural elderly were financially independent as against 28.94 percent of their urban counterparts (National Sample Survey, 1991). Of course, the situation varies from state to state. In Maharashtra, the dependence of rural elderly was 33 per cent as against 46 per cent among the urban elderly (Dandekar, 1993). Besides, the aged females, especially those residing in the urban areas, were most dependent (Dandekar, 1996).

Analysis of the labour force participation among the elderly is important from the point of view of understanding their economic dependence given the fact of inadequate social security. The predominant rural character of the population coupled with opportunities for insufficient wage and salaried employment compel people to prolong their working lives as long as, is physically possible even after retirement. Even in the case of self-employment, economic compulsions force many to continue work as long as they are able to do so though perhaps at a reduced pace. Analysis of the employment pattern of the working elderly shows that, on the whole, their work participation rates were on the decrease between 1961-91 irrespective of rural or urban residence though the work participation of the elderly continues to be remarkably higher in rural areas compared to urban areas.

Participation rate among elderly persons declined by 10 units between 1961 and 1981, the reduction was 9 units and 7 units respectively for rural and urban areas. Between 1981 and 1991, the decline is only 1 per cent. Detailed analysis indicates that more elderly men participate in economic activities than women. This may partly be due to the definitional problems related to women's work in the census (Leela Gulati, Irudaya Rajan and Ramalingam, 1997). One-third of elderly males continue to work even beyond 80 years (Table 2.13). Surprisingly, however, the share of old age workers in agriculture has been on the increase over time, both in rural and urban areas. Almost 80 per cent of the aged workers in India worked in the agricultural sector in 1991.

Detailed investigation into the phenomenon indicates that around 62 per cent of elderly males work as cultivators whereas 70 per cent of females work as agricultural labourers. If elderly persons participate in economic activities beyond 60 years of age, could we conclude that they are dependent in the old age. For the first time in the 1981 census, the data on main workers was classified by marital status. It showed that 58 per cent of widowed elderly worked as main workers in rural areas and 69 per cent in urban areas. Confronted with the burden of maintenance themselves, elderly persons in India continue to work even after reaching 60 years of age. In one of the group discussions among the rural elderly in India, we were told, "for us there is only one retirement, not from work, but from the world" (see Irudaya Rajan, Mishra, Sarma, 1999).

Indian census also provides economic data on non-workers by categories such as household workers, beggars, students, pensioners, rentiers and others. Though there are problems with defining non-workers, some crude observations can be made. As of 1991, around 40 percent of Indian women were involved in household duties indicating their active participation in maintaining and caring for their children and grand children. Another 5 per cent are pensioners, 0.5

Table 2.13: Work Participation Rate by Sex among 60 Plus, 70 Plus and 80 Plus Elderly, 1991.

States	Males			Females		
	60+	70+	80+	60+	70+	80+
Arunchal Pradesh	74.9	56.1	40.2	46.5	27.5	17.7
Assam	64.1	48.3	34.4	14.2	7.9	5.5
Bihar	67.5	50.8	41.3	12.1	7.0	6.2
Goa	41.4	24.7	17.7	10.8	4.7	2.8
Gujarat	49.6	31.1	24.9	14.3	6.8	5.3
Haryana	53.8	35.6	21.0	6.6	3.2	2.0
Himachal Pradesh	65.1	46.8	27.9	27.8	14.3	7.8
Karnataka	56.7	37.5	25.3	18.1	8.9	5.9
Kerala	45.7	26.7	16.3	9.6	3.8	2.4
Madhya Pradesh	65.5	47.5	38.1	26.2	13.8	10.1
Maharashtra	54.4	33.7	20.8	23.7	10.8	6.4
Manipur	70.2	50.3	32.1	44.9	25.3	14.5
Meghalaya	77.1	62.7	49.4	41.3	26.6	17.6
Mizoram	66.9	41.7	24.9	38.8	19.7	9.8
Nagaland	82.7	71.8	58.2	69.5	54.5	38.5
Orissa	61.1	38.7	26.1	12.6	6.3	4.9
Rajasthan	53.7	33.4	18.5	2.5	1.4	0.9
Sikkim	73.1	53.8	38.2	31.8	18.4	12.1
Tamil Nadu	57.1	39.8	29.8	21.3	11.5	7.8
West Bengal	54.0	36.3	32.4	6.5	3.2	2.6
Andman and Nicobar	60.4	47.3	35.6	10.7	6.2	4.2
Chandigarh	33.2	20.8	14.6	2.7	1.5	1.1
Dadar & Nagar Haveli	66.2	44.6	35.4	35.6	21.3	8.5
Daman & Diu	50.6	33.6	21.5	15.9	8.3	3.0
Delhi	39.0	25.6	19.4	3.6	2.0	1.6
Pondicherry	43.3	27.4	16.2	9.5	5.1	3.1
All India	**60.5**	**42.3**	**31.7**	**16.1**	**8.2**	**5.7**

per cent work as beggars and 0.1 percent live in institutions for the aged and indigient. In a recent study conducted by the senior author of this paper, it was observed that there were 134 old age homes providing accomodation for 5000 elderly in Kerala (Irudaya Rajan, 2000). Only 56 per cent of women and 67 per cent of men were reported as dependents. They are the ones need social assistance and support in their old age. According to the same census, the number of persons who required social assistance were found to be very low in West Bengal, followed by Tamil Nadu and Gujarat; the highest number was reported in Haryana, Punjab and Rajasthan. For instance, the highest number of pensioners were reported in West Bengal, followed by Tamil Nadu and Gujarat. Surprisingly, only 23 per cent of men and 4 per cent of women receive pensions in Kerala. The highest number of women pensioners are found in Tamil Nadu, followed by Gujarat and West Bengal.

Implications of Ageing on Policy

The family as a single unit is likely to change. The old age dependency will increase faster than the decline in child dependency. It will require lot of adjustment at the family level to accommodate and care for the elderly. While the daughters and daughters-in-law replacing their role as care-givers to their parents by working outside home, a new challenge for elderly care will be posed. Day-care centres, geriatric hospitals and old age homes are likely to play a major role in the living arrangements for the elderly. For instance, Kerala had in 1999 134 old age homes which accommodated more than 5000 persons; of which, 35 per cent consisted of males and 65 per cent of females (Irudaya Rajan, 2000).

The elderly are likely to become more vulnerable in the absence of familial support network; hence they need a strong social security system. The current elderly who have not made adequate provision for old age may be in for a great deal of frustration at the hands of their children during the old age. Social security measures for the prospective elderly may thus become imperative.

The increasing number and proportion of elderly will have a direct impact on the demand for health services. Currently, the Government of India runs various health programs targeted primarily at the needs of mothers and children. Primary health care system is not geared up to meet the future challenges arising from an increase in chronic diseases. Conditions like hypertension and diabetes, which have higher incidence among the aged, will pose an increasing burden to the elderly themselves and to their families. Mobilising additional resources for geriatric care will emerge as a major responsibility of health care providers in countries like India. Achieving this without affecting maternal and pediatric care will be a challenge.

Notes and References

Bass A Scott, Robert Morris and Masato Oka (eds). 1996. Public Policy and Old Age Revolution in Japan, The Haworth Press, USA.

Dak, T.M. and M.L. Sharma, 1987, Changing Status of the Aged in North Indian Villages. in M.L. Sharma and T.M. Dak (Eds). *Aging in India*, Ajanta publications (India), New Delhi, pp. 43-55.

Dandekar, K., 1993, The Aged, Their Problems and Social Intervention in Maharashtra. *Economic and Political Weekly,* Vol.XXVII No. 23 June 5, pp. 1188-94.

Dandekar, K., 1996, *The Elderly in India*, Sage Publications, New Delhi.

Desai, K G., 1985, Situation of the Aged in India, *Journal of the Indian Anthropological Society*, Volume 20, No. 3, pp. 201-09.

Grigsby, J., 1993, Paths for Future Population Aging, *The Gerontologist*, Volume 31, No. 2, April, pp. 195-203.

Guilmoto Z Christophe and S Irudaya Rajan, 1998, Regional Heterogeneity and Fertility Behaviour in India. Working Paper No. 290, Centre for Development Studies, Trivandrum.

Irudaya Rajan, S., 1994. China's One Child Policy: Implication for Population Aging. *Economic and Political Weekly*, Volume XXIX, No.38, September 17, pp. 2502-06.

Irudaya Rajan S, U S Mishra and P S Sarma. 1996. INDIA: National Aging Trends. pp. 79-104 in United Nations. 1996. *Life Long Preparation for Old Age in Asia and the Pacific*. United Nations, New York. ST/ ESCAP/1684.

Irudaya Rajan S, U S Mishra and P S Sarma, 1999, *India's Elderly: Burden or Challenge?* Sage Publications, New Delhi/Thousand Oaks/London.

Irudaya Rajan, S, U S Mishra and P S Sarma, 2000, Aging in India: Retrospect and Prospect. *Indian Social Science Review*, Volume 2, No.1.

Irudaya Rajan, S, U S Mishra and Mala Ramanathan, 1993, Two Child Family in India: Is it Realistic? *International Family Planning Perspectives,* Vol 19, No 4, pp. 125-128 & 154.

Irudaya Rajan and Mishra, 1995. Defining Old Age: An Indian Assessment, *Bold*, Journal of United Nations Institute on Aging, Malta, Volume 5, No.4, pp. 31-35.

Irudaya Rajan, S and K C Zachariah, 1998, Long Term Implications of Low Fertility in Kerala, India. *Asia-Pacific Population Journal*, Volume 13, No. 13, September, pp. 41-66.

Irudaya Rajan, 1999. Aging and Social Security, Chapter 3, pp.49-71 in B A Prakash (eds). Kerala's Economic Development: Issues and Problems, Sage Publications, New Delhi.

Irudaya Rajan, S., 2000, Home Away from Home: A Survey of Oldage Homes and Inmates in Kerala, Centre for Development Studies Working Paper No. 305, Thiruvananthapuram.

Kaur Malkit, R P Grover and Kusul Aggarwal, 1987, Socio-economic Profile of the Rural Aged, In M.L. Sharma and T.M. Dak (Eds). *Aging in India*, Ajanta publications (India), New Delhi, pp. 67-75.

Leela Gulati, S Irudaya Rajan and A Ramalingam, 1997, Women and Work in Kerala: A Comparison of the 1981 and 1991 censuses, *Indian Journal of Gender Studies*, Volume 4, No. 2, pp. 231-52.

Mari Bhat, P N and S Irudaya Rajan, 1990, Demographic Transition in Kerala Revisited. *Economic and Political Weekly*, Vol XXV, Nos 35 & 36, September 1-8, pp. 1957-1980.

Mari Bhat, P N, K Navaneetham and S Irudaya Rajan, 1995, Maternal Mortality in India: Estimates from a Regression Model. *Studies in Family Planning*, Volume. 26, Number 4, July/August, pp. 217-232.

Mari Bhat, P N, 1992, Changing Demography of Elderly in India, *Current Science*, Volume 63, No.8, October 25, pp. 440-48.

Myers, G.C., 1986, Cross-National Patterns and Trends in Marital Status Among the Elderly. Paper presented to the conference on Aged populations and the Gray Revolution, Universite Catholique de Louvain, Belgium, October.

Nandal, D.S., R.S. Khatri and R.S. Kadian, 1987, Aging problems in the structural context. In M.L. Sharma and T.M. Dak (Eds), *Aging in India*, Ajanta publications (India), New Delhi, pp. 106-16.

National Sample Survey Organisation, 1991, Socio-Economic Profile of the Aged persons: NSS 42nd Round (July 1986 - June 1987), *Sarvekshana*, Vol.15 No.2, New Delhi.

Punia Deepa and M L Sharma, 1987, Family Life of Rural Aged Women, In M.L. Sharma and T.M. Dak (Eds). *Aging in India*, Ajanta publications (India) New Delhi, pp. 57-66.

Shah, V.P., 1993, *The Elderly in Gujarat*, Department of Sociology, Gujarat University, Ahmedabad (Mimeographed).

Singh Kanta, Raj Singh and M.L. Sharma (1987). Problems of Aged Women in Haryana. In M.L. Sharma and T.M. Dak (Eds). *Aging in India*, Ajanta publications (India), New Delhi, pp. 134-144.

Sudha, S and S Irudaya Rajan, 1999, Female Demographic Disadvantage in India 1981-1991, Role of Sex Selective Abortions and Female Infanticide, Development and Change, Volume 30, No.3, pp. 585-618.

Treas, J. and Logue, B., 1986, Economic Development and the Older Population, *Population and Development Review*, Vol. 12(4), pp. 645-673.

United Nations, 1998, *World Population Projections to 2150*, Department of Economic and Social Affairs, Population Division, New York.

World Bank, 1994, *Averting the Old Age Crisis: Policies to Protect the Old and Promote Growth*, Oxford University Press, Oxford.

Zachariah, K C and Irudaya Rajan, 1997, Kerala's Demographic Transition: An Overview. Chapter 1, pp. 17-29 in K C Zachariah and S Irudaya Rajan (eds) 1997, *Kerala's Demographic Transition: Determinants and Consequences*, Sage Publications, New Delhi.

3

The Wrinkled Face of the Passing Years

JOHN WOODALL*

Social security is itself a multi-dimensional subject, not least in its application to providing for the relevant needs of the elderly members of the population, whether those provisions be in cash or in kind. Over many years, the different facets of such provision have been developed, whether by way of saving for old age through provident funds or pension schemes, or relevant benefits-in-kin, such as the provision of residential homes for the elderly or the types of specialized health care which may be needed by senior citizens. Over time, these provisions have developed in order to replace the older modes of support for the elderly, through family and kinship structures. These themselves of course reflect traditional and cultural values of respect, but adapted in a rather inadequate way to the trends of movement of many workers to urban and centralized workplaces (including the agricultural plantations), away from their extended-family homes.

Nevertheless, a number of issues have been raised in recent years, focusing on the consequences of increasing longevity and the consequent impact on the financial resources required to provide pension and other long-term benefits through social security arrangements. These issues have been cast in the form of a world-wide debate as to the 'affordability' of social security for old age, particularly in conditions where economic pressures, often associated with the processes of 'globalisation', 'liberalization' and increasingly 'informal' modes of employment, are more evident than hitherto. Many commentators have drawn the conclusion that 'Pension Reform' is necessary, and in many countries this has had a direct impact, at the political level, on the development of policies towards social security and social protection.

---

* Senior Specialist in Social Security, ILO-SAAT, New Delhi The opinions expressed are personal, and should not be taken as any statement of ILO policy.

In the opinion of the author, much of the argument which is presented in the context of the debate on 'pension reform' reflects nothing so much as muddled thinking – the "wrinkles in our minds", perhaps, to which the French essayist of the title quotation alluded some hundreds of years ago. Social security schemes are not created in social vaccum, and are not created simply as vehicles for financial and investment purposes. They are designed to provide appropriate support for those whose ability to generate their own income (and access to health care) is lost, whether temporarily (as in the case of sickness benefits) or permanently, as in the case of those who retire at the end of their normal working lives.

If, then, we take as a fundamental premise – as, in the author's submission, we should – then the details of policy regarding old-age social security can be developed in a logical and coherent manner, taking account of the prevailing conditions of the country and time. A number of such aspects are discussed in this paper, which attempts to highlight those which are especially topical, but it is not intended by any means to provide a comprehensive summary of all of the relevant issues. Economic and financial conditions are, of course, extremely important, but it seems altogether inappropriate that these should be allowed to dictate the 'philosophical' or constitutional basis on which a country chooses to make social provisions of this kind.

In laying out the framework for such discussion, it is important to note that provision for old age may be made in many ways, including:

1. nationally-mandated–social security and social protection agreements;
2. community schemes;
3. individually initiated savings and insurance arrangements.

Some recent, theoretical work on social security schemes (in general, and not simply relating to old age) has taken, as a starting point, the concept of 'social risk management'. It is valuable to consider those aspects of old age provision which can in fact be analysed in terms of measurable risk. However, most of us would consider, or at least allow ourselves to hope, that old age is a contingency which is more or less certain to come about. From this point of view, 'society' should, it may be strongly argued, make relevant provision for its senior members on an equally assured basis.

The author's views on this subject have developed in the course of working with ILO in a number of countries, in particular those of South Asia.

See, for example, 'Social Risk Management: A New Conceptual framework for Social Protection, and Beyond' – Robert Holzmann and Steen Jorgensen, World Bank, February 2000.

Ageing Around the World

The most striking feature to which social protection systems around the world must address themselves, in current times, is the increasing longevity of the populations in all but a very few countries. In order to analyse the impact on formal social security schemes, it is more important to consider the expectation of life (of an 'average' individual) at some particular point of middle age, i.e., age 50 or 60, rather than the expectation of life at birth. However, it is clear that on average, both men and women are living longer than in former years; whether the differential expectation of life as between the sexes is increasing or decreasing is less clear. However, it is observed that, in general, those in their later years tend to be fitter and more active than hitherto, leading to considerable discussion as to their ability to remain economically active to advanced ages in a manner which has hardly been thought of in the past.

A second trend which is clear from demographic analyses around the world is the decease in fertility rates – a trend which has not developed in quite such a universal manner as has the increase in longevity, but which is nevertheless widespread and accelerating. In a number of western countries, and now Asian countries also, this trend has developed to the point at which it seems probable that the total populations, although still increasing at present, will begin to reduce in the foreseeable future.

The combined result of (mainly) these two trends together is that the proportion of elderly persons in the population of many countries is now increasing very sharply, and will continue to do so for many years into the future. In particular, the ratio of the elderly to those who form the active workforce is increasing in a comparable manner (if not necessarily at the same rate). Most social security retirement benefit schemes, have been designed on the basis of financing plans, including rates of contribution to be paid by employers and employees which rely on the prospect that there will be 'sufficient' worker-members, and hence contribution income, to provide the benefits for the expected numbers of retired pensioners. The kind of instability in the age profile of the members has certainly brought about difficulties in maintaining appropriate financial and funding system in such schemes.

In the relatively 'developed' countries of Europe, North America, Japan and Australia, the combined result of these trends has been to slow population growth (and to halt it entirely in some of these countries). However, the numbers of those in the oldest age brackets has continued to increase, and consequently the proportion of the elderly in the total population – the old-age dependency ratio- is increasing very rapidly indeed. At the same time, the decline in birth rates has been such that the numbers of children, and their proportion in the total population, the youth dependency ratio, has also stabilized or begun to fall. In some countries, there is now a possibility of releasing some resources previously devoted to the young, from sectors such as education and paediatric health care, and redirecting them to the needs of the elderly. This is not, however a straightforward process, as those who are trained as teachers, for example, cannot necessarily be easily redeployed in the care of old people.

In most of the countries of Africa, the demographic transition is certainly at a different stage, and may be following a different trajectory, to that of the developed countries. Improving health parameters (at least in the years before the impact of HIV/AIDS on the morbidity and mortality statistics in these countries became apparent) had contributed strongly to increasing longevity, although fertility rates although showing signs of falling, perhaps have not yet reached the point where the total numbers of children are falling noticeably. These countries, then, are experiencing steep rises in the both the youth and old-age dependency ratios, which, taken together with their stresses economic circumstances have resulted in the tendency of governments to spread resources very thinly and in generally poor levels of social provision for both groups.

Across Asia, the circumstances of different countries vary widely, reflecting a wide variety of experience in economic development, and also a variety of cultural factors. In countries where urbanization of the population is not marked, it has been easier to bring the benefits of better health services to greater numbers of people than is the case where the population has remained widely spread across rural areas. The impact of patterns of diseases (such as HIV/AIDS) remains somewhat unclear. However, the statistics indicate that many of these countries are entering the demographic transition to low birth rates and long life expectancy, and in a few countries such as Sri Lanka, this trend has progressed strongly.

In due course, it seems overwhelmingly likely that all countries will experience a demographic transition of similar nature. However, there will be a wide variation in the speed at which the transition develops, and some countries will have at their disposal a longer period of years in which to plan to meet the new set of needs reflected int eh changing age profile of their people. Their challenge will be to use that period effectively and not to 'waste' the opportunity to develop policies and strategies in good time to meet those needs.

Traditional Provisions for the Elderly

Historically, of course, the needs of the elderly were provided for by their families; in the predominantly rural and agrarian setting in which most people lived until relatively recently, it was natural to deal with the needs of not only the elderly, but also the young the sick and any other needy or incapacitated family members in this way. The situation changed radically when workers began to move to the large towns and cities, to take up work in the large factories, stores and other business enterprises established in those centers. In Europe and North America, this resulted in a more or less complete social transformation, which took place quite quickly, beginning some three hundred years ago. In the less developed countries, the process has begun later, and has been less complete, with a much larger proportion of the population remaining and working 'on the land'. Nevertheless, the move to the urban areas has been very significant, and has greatly weakened the family ties on which those in need could rely. These are the basic circumstances in which the need for formal social security schemes became apparent and in which schemes of the 'traditional' type have been designed, to meet the circumstances of those who suffer the loss of their income (or need access to health services) on meeting with a range of specifically designated contingencies. This, then, is the background to the specification in instruments such as, notably, International Labor Convention No.102 (of 1952, concerning Minimum Standards of Social Security).

The protection envisaged for those whose income-earning capacity has eroded due to age is the payment of lifetime pensions, preferably related in a defined manner to the same individual's general level of earnings before retirement. Nevertheless, many social security schemes have been set up around the world as provident funds, which generally provide benefits in the form of lump sums. Such schemes tend to be well valued by their members, despite the theoretical disadvantages compared with pension schemes. This particular source of controversy and debate is certainly important, but may, perversely, tend to blur the focus on the basic need to provide for the upkeep of the elderly.

In the nature of a provident fund, the monies contributed by and on behalf of the members can be identified with each individual, and accordingly it is usual that the funds be accounted for as such; in other words a provident fund is (in most circumstances) naturally of the type of scheme described as 'funded'. A pension scheme need not be formulated in the same way, and may be either funded or unfunded, of the type often labeled 'pay-as-you-go'.

We should note her that what is at issue is the sharing of the country's total current, consumable resources between the active, working population and those who are not presently working, more significantly the elderly and the young. This principle is not changed, whatever the financial arrangements underlying a scheme to provide benefits to retiring or retired workers, and whatever notional financial rights may be assigned on the basis of individuals' contributions. This, accordingly, underpins at least a major part of the fundamental justification for the social basis of income support.

In this brief overview of the 'traditional' approach to social security provision, one other aspect which may be highlighted, and which may well be seen as outmoded in modern conditions, is the conceptual 'model' of a typical family as supported by a single, archetypically male, breadwinner. This is reflected in the provisions in many schemes for benefits to be paid on the death of a member, whether in the form of a lump sum or pension annuity, but only to the widow or dependants of a man, much more rarely to the male dependant widower of a female breadwinner.

What Are the Perceptions of the Elderly Themselves?

In seeking appropriate policies and strategies for the future, whether in particular countries or on a global basis, it is clear that, at an early stage, we should understand as far as possible the way in which the elderly themselves view the relevant issues.

Firstly, we should note the worldwide trend for groups within the population to identify themselves and to assert their needs and aspirations in terms of rights. If this conceptual framework is admitted, then there are several relevant 'rights' which may be readily identified, including, in particular: the right to equality of treatment with younger segments of population, which might imply, for example, that the national government would be required to give equal weight to the economic and welfare interests of the elderly as against the "active" workforce; the right to provision of benefits through social security.

The 'right to social security' has a variety of cannotations. Indeed, aspects, at least, of such a right may be enshrined in the national constitution.* Most readily recognized, however, is the assertion that, having served the country through working lifetime, those who have retired have in fact earned the 'right' to financial support in their old age. That right may well be expressed in a measurable way, in terms of the financial accumulation of contributions paid, during, while actually working, by or on behalf of each individual. This argument brings us to the concept of insurance: the payment of contributions (or, in the technical jargon of insurers, 'premiums') ensures the subsequent right to claim benefits when defined 'risk' conditions, or contingencies are fulfilled. However, it is important, in analysing the operation of a social security scheme, to distinguish between forms of insurance in which either:

(a) payments into the insurance scheme or arrangement premiums are charged on a basis which is assessed in relation to the risk which each insured individual brings to the 'risk pool'; or
(b) payments are made by the insured members (contributions) on a basis which is assessed 'socially' with at least some reference toe ach individual's ability to pay.

The latter type of arrangement is generally referred to as 'social insurance'; because the arrangement is not, from an individual's point of view (in general) prospectively neutral in financially-costed risk

---

* The Constitution of India does not refer to the term 'Social Security' as such, but Article 41 does provide that "The State shall, within the limits of its economic capacity and development, make effective provision for securing the right to work, to education and to public assistance in cases of unemployment, old age, sickness and disablement, and in other cases of underserved want".

(or 'actuarial') terms, such schemes cannot usually be arranged on a basis of membership which is completely voluntary, and must depend on some degree of compulsion, which in turn must normally be mandated at a national level, or alternatively may rely on the type of 'solidarity' which may in some circumstances be possible through an appropriate society, co-operative, or trade union.

The former type of insurance, which is readily possible on the basis of voluntary participation, is that normally transacted by commercial insurance companies, and may be termed 'commercial' insurance, although many non-profit making societies and so-called 'mutual' companies also operate on this basis, which itself is sometimes terms that of 'mutuality'.

Lastly, for the purposes of this overview, we may consider the degree to which, in a growing economy, those who number the elderly and retired should participate financially in the general growth of prosperity. This, of course, raises many complex social questions, but there is an aspect of particular importance to those amongst the elderly who are paid pensions. This relates to the degree to which the real value, in other words the purchasing power, of each unit of pension may be protected against the diminution of value which results from the process of inflation. Most schemes and countries will try to provide for some degree of 'cost-of-living' protection, but there is great deal of variation as to whether this is done on the basis of an automatic formula, applied at least once a year, or on an adhoc basis when the government deems that needs have become pressing and that there are sufficient funds available. The approach of applying an automatic formula may also be applied in different ways, with the annual amount of pension benefits being increased in proportion to an index of either:

(a) price increases; or

(b) wage and salary increases.

The impact on the share of 'national wealth' allocated to pensioners can vary quite dramatically with this choice.

What May Be Needed In Modern Conditions

The author would suggest that the appropriate starting point for establishing a national policy perspective for the financial (and related needs) of the elderly is one which pays regard to the this elderly group as full members of society. The traditional values of respect for these senior members need to be reinforced, rather than displaced or simply forgotten.

Within this perspective, it should be possible to establish a national commitment to provide for the elderly, as a right, and on the basis of the contribution which they have already made to society through their working lifetimes, whether or not employed in any formal setting.

It must be recognized, of course, that there is a very wide variation in the capacities of different countries to provide adequately for those of their people who cannot sufficiently support themselves. The reasons for this are diverse, but predominantly reflect countries differing economic circumstances. Nations such as India have faced difficulties in meeting many of the pressing needs of the vast population, and not only those of the elderly or other prospective beneficiaries of the social security system. The impact of globalization, and the pressures to liberalise financial systems have, regardless of the extent to which the effect on the wider economy may be beneficial or otherwise, brought with them the need for adjustments in the existing systems of social security which are by no means easy to achieve, and whose effects may not be felt equitably by the members in general.

In these circumstances, it is certainly not easy to establish policies in regard to social protection for the elderly which will both meet the objective needs and at the same time command strong public support. However, it is suggested here that if the optimum course is to be found, this will be achieved by focusing firstly on the purpose of establishing systems of social protection in the first place, that is, to meet clearly identifiable social needs, and not to treat the relevant institutions simply or primarily as components of the financial infrastructure of the country.

To do so tends strongly to lead to bringing social security institutions into the framework of short-term economic planning, which is clearly inappropriate for institutions whose task is to provide income security in the long term – indeed the longest of terms by comparison with an individual's potential lifetime. Social security both requires a long term perspective if it is to fulfil its purpose, but at the same time the experience accumulated globally in the design and administration of such schemes over many decades can provide the relevant conceptual tools for such long term planning.

Accordingly, the need to provide pensions should be recognized as a long term commitment, even if it is not currently possible to finance these adequately at the present time. The elderly should be seen as entitled to an appropriate share of national income, and the real value of that share should be protected against the depredations of inflation, preferably on an income-related rather than price-determined basis. In this regard, it is relevant to note that price indices appropriate to the 'average' consumer may be quite inappropriate to the elderly.

The Capacity To Work Into Old Age

Concurrently with the general increase seen around the world in life expectancy, the health and fitness of the elderly has tended to improve, if not universally then certainly on average, in recent years. This has reflected in some cases in better health care facilities, but more importantly much higher levels of awareness amongst the public of the means to maintain their own general health.

In the case of workers who have spent a lifetime in difficult, dangerous or unpleasant occupations, the result may be a wish to enjoy a longer and healthier retirement than their forefathers. However, there is a growing category of workers in certain occupations who both wish to continue to work into relatively old age and retain adequate capacities, both physical and mental, to do so.

In these circumstances, it is necessary to consider whether workers should not be required, as has been the case to date, to retire on reaching a certain fixed age. This is a question which has, perhaps, been given additional prominence by the different retirement ages which are enforced in many schemes for men and women, so leading to instances of gender inequality which may be more exaggerated than necessary. In India, the age at which retirement should take place has already become a matter of controversy, in the future it may be necessary to face up to the question as to whether this concept of retirement can itself be maintained.

Employment Considerations

There are a number of factors, which interact in rather complex ways, which policy makers must take into consideration in contemplating the prospect that significant numbers of older workers will retain their jobs into relatively old age.

Prospectively, such a trend should lead to lower (old-age) dependency ratios that would otherwise be the case, with a strongly beneficial effect on the contribution capacity and financial balance of formal social security schemes. However, this would only come about if the total quantum of (formal or organized) employment were to increase to the extent needed to absorb the increasing total number of those who seek opportunities.

The experience in many, if not most, countries in recent years has been that employment opportunities are generally insufficient, at least in the formal or organized economy, and growth of employment has been marked only in the relatively informal sectors, which are generally outside the scope or organized social security schemes. Policy makers have often drawn the conclusion that to allow workers to retain their jobs into old age would exacerbate the shortage of opportunities for those entering the workforce at younger ages, and that, indeed, retirement ages should be reduced in some cases. however, it is nto at all clear that this approach has been generally correct.

The removal of older workers from the workforce has not always, by any means, been accompanied by the absorption of young workers therein. The 'employability' of the latter, in occupations which increasingly require literacy, numeracy and related skills is increasingly dependant on standards of education which have not universally kept pace with the relevant requirements. In addition, such a simplistic approach to the very serious problem of matching available workers against available jobs fails to attribute significant value to the accumulated work experience and skills which should be acquired over a working lifetime. These considerations point in conflicting directions, and certainly do not lead to easy policy conclusions. Perhaps the only clear indication in this regard is the need for the type of economic growth which can lead to greater employment in decent and properly protected jobs.

Financial And Funding Considerations

It is not the intention of this paper to examine in detail the financial implications of the issues which have been raised. However, in order to fill as completely as possible the canvas representing the field of decisions to be addressed by policy makers, the main elements are noted below, in qualitative rather than quantitative terms.

Firstly, we should note that the provision of pension benefits which may be paid 'too early' entails costs for social security schemes which can be very high indeed when expressed in terms of contributions rates; this is because not only are pensions paid for additional years, but contributions are received in respect of such individuals over shorter than 'normal' working lives. Conversely, an increase in the age at which members retire, individually or on average, can have a much more than proportionate effect in easing the long term contribution rates required for funding retirement costs.

Secondly, it may be noted that the 'capitalized' costs of pension 'annuities', as measured actuarially, are much more sensitive than is often realized to the rate of earnings on the invested assets which may be used to support them. This factor is of considerable significance in the type of (defined contribution) pension scheme where individual members; accumulations of contributions are 'annuitised' through insurance institutions; the impact in 'self-insured' or 'self-administered' schemes may be less evident on a year by year basis, but is nevertheless real. Accordingly, it is important to ensure that the manner in which the accumulated funds of a scheme (other than one financed on a pay-as-you-go basis) are invested is fully appropriate.

Financial and investment conditions may change quite rapidly, and those who are responsible for the investment of funds must respond rapidly and appropriately to such changes. One aspect of this need is to provide appropriate and timely advice to those who are statutorily responsible when it becomes apparent that changes are needed to the main financial parameters of a scheme, notably the benefit formulae and contribution rates.

In each of these regards, it is notable in schemes around the world that those responsible for financial administration tend to exercise considerable caution in their decision making. In general terms, this is of course appropriate. However, the risks to be avoided are not always entirely obvious. In particular, the impact of inflation at even faily modest levels and its destructive effect on the real value of benefits specified in money terms presents a very real risk to the financial capacity of a scheme to fulfil its designed purpose, the severity of which is too often overlooked.

Policy Implications

The following indicates in very broad terms the range of issues which stand to be addressed by those responsible for maintaining and developing national policies in regard to provision of social benefits for the elderly.

The first is to recognize the changing balance, in present day conditions, between considerations of:

(a) longevity
(b) income needs
(c) increasing capacity to work into old age and
(d) increasing desire by at least a segment of the older workforce to continue working.

The next is to promote public awareness of the relevant issues, and on that basis mandate in the long term is the capacity cannot be mobilized in the short term financial support as appropriate, on the basis of an appropriate degree of social sharing of the national income.

In addition, consideration should be given to support through relevant benefits "in kind", of which the best known "traditional" social security benefit is health care (which in turn must be appropriate to the needs of the elderly), but which increasingly may include such items as sheltered accommodation and nutritional support.

Summary

We live in a time of change the impact of which is felt with great strength on social provisions for the elderly members of each nation's society. In the past, support for this segment of society has reflected long held values, notably of respect, entrenched in national cultures. In the frenetic pace of modern, increasingly urban lifestyles, it is easy for such values to be overlooked, but it is important that they should not be forgotten or extinguished.

Newer values of solidarity, which may buttress or substitute for family and kinship ties, are also under pressure in materialistic societies, but must also be maintained and reinforced.

All around the world, societies face difficult adjustments to face the economic trends of globalisation, urbanisation and increasingly informal or unorganized modes of employment, and the demographic trends which are leading to dramatically increased dependency ratios. The need to balance the claims of the dependant segments of population with those of the producers of current wealth and income demand clear analysis and leadership from the leaders of society.

We shall all, we hope, number ourselves amongst the elderly in due course, but will hope to live out a ripe old age in conditions of financial comfort, however modest; this reflection should guide the manner in which, today, we address the problems of those who have already reached that seniority.

Recent Development in Old-age, Invalidity and Survivors' Insurance

GENERAL SECRETARY, ISSA, GENEVA

Public pension schemes in many developed countries are reaching maturity, and in some cases, are paying large benefits to those reaching retirement age. The poverty problem is less apparent than before in developed countries, but nevertheless remains a source of concern for part of the retired population.[1] The pension schemes in these countries face several economic, demographic and social challenges, particularly connected to the aging of the populations, to the important changes occurring in the labor market and in family structures, which will probably continue to influence, for a long time to come, the evolution of the income of retired persons.

Among all the problems which exert considerable pressure on public pension schemes in developed countries and lead them towards the path of reform, the paramount one is the difficulty of ensuring the viability of these schemes in the medium and long term. Some countries are also concerned about the weakness of the system concerning the legal age of retirement and its implications. The issue of the adequacy of the level of benefits paid upon retirement, the possibilities of widening the scope of coverage of the schemes and increasing the motivation to work through an appropriate organization of the pension system, are also among the priorities pointed out by certain countries.

In some developed countries, the increase in the level of contributions and/or a tightening of the requirements concerning occupational careers, in order to be entitled to the same level of benefits, as well as an increase in the age of retirement, are mong the aspects targeted by the reform. Many countries are actively involved in reducing or canceling the financial incentives of early retirement, even if some exceptions may be observed. A greater role is being given to private pension schemes in order to avoid public schemes being the only solution, and, in some instances to supplement the pensions paid by the public schemes. Some countries have set up measures with the objective of encouraging workers to work longer, other measures are intended as incentives to slow down the activities of workers, in order to gradually prepare them for final retirement. Conversely, still other countries discourage retired pensioners from simultaneously exercising an occupation (Kalisch and Aman, 1997).

For many countries of Latin America, and of Central and Eastern Europe, the most urgent problems involve the collection of contributions, the scope of coverage and the financial viability of the schemes. These problems constitute the basis of the most important reforms undertaken in these countries, where emphasis is placed on individual accounts and on funded pensions systems with defined contributions. In developing countries in the Asian and Pacific region, where most of the existing pension systems covered until recently only the workers of the public sector and/or enterprises situated in urban zones, the main aspect of the reforms has been to extend the scope of coverage of the pension systems (Devereux, 1998).

In the case of sub-Saharan Africa, economic restructuring (consisting of measures known as stabilization and structural adjustment) undertaken in several countries advocate a policy for the short and medium term of allocating limited resources to social programmes in order to provide the maximum amount of resources to projects aimed at accelerating economic growth. The implementation of these measures particularly those leading to the penalizing of enterprises considered insufficiently profitable, has led up to now to the lowering of the level of employment due to cuts in manpower and the closing down of enterprises. This resulted in a reduction in the volume of contributions collected by social security institutions, which are thus deprived of their main sources of income. The combined effect of this reduction in the volume of contributions and of the increase in life expectancy makes even more difficult maintaining the financial balance of the pension schemes in the medium and long term. In addition, in many countries, the reserves of the social security institutions were sometimes lost because of the liquidation of banks following economic restructuring or because of loans made by the State which were not reimbursed (ISSA, 1994, 1995).

The other problems faced by countries in this region are especially linked to the difficulty of collecting contributions, to the insufficient skills in the different fields of specialization in social security management, as well as the insufficient use of actuarial analyses as a decision making tool.

On the level of African social security institutions, the perspectives for the future are mainly focused on strengthening the control of the employers in order to insure, if possible, all salaries workers; adopting all the measures likely to facilitate the collection of contributions and the control of the implementation of legislation in this field by the employers; gradually implementing appropriate statistical techniques which would allow forward-looking management and periodic actuarial studies developed on the basis of reliable data: and promoting an appropriate policy for the training and specialization of staff. In the legislative sphere, the modifications envisaged would consist in raising the legal age of retirement (which is currently 55 years in many cases) combined with an extension of the period providing entitlement to a full pension (currently equal to 15 years in most cases), as well as an extension of the coverage to more segments of the population.

Aging of the Population and Pension Systems

According to current data and to forecasts made in several studies, the aging of populations will represent a major challenge for the pension systems of many Western countries in the coming years. The problem is nevertheless not global, as yet, even though current trends suggest that this may become the case in the future.

The rate of old age dependency, commonly defined as the percentage of the population aged 65 years or more in relation to the number of persons aged between 15 and 64 years, is the variable usually used to measure the phenomenon of aging.[2] The two most determining variable for forecasts on the demographic structure, namely the mortality rate and the fertility rate, are evolving in such a way as to accelerate the aging phenomenon in many industrialized countries: in some countries like Germany, Italy, or Japan, according to the forecasts, the rate of old age dependency will more than double between 1995 and 2050 (Jollans, 1997).

Let us consider the case of a pay-as-you-go pension scheme, and adopt the simplistic hypothesis that all persons in the category 15 years to 64 years contribute to the scheme and that all persons aged 65 years or older are the beneficiaries.[3] Two times the dependency rate would call for two times the contribution rate, all other factors being equal. This explains the importance of the notion of the dependency rate, which has the objective of providing an estimate of the number of aged persons (who are unproductive in economic terms) who will have to be supported by the output produced by the active population. This usually has an impact on the whole economy, which suggests that it also has an impact on the private funded pension schemes.

The demographic aging issue is making many pay-as-you-go schemes wonder as to how they will solve the problem of financial imbalance which will arise in the medium and long term. In some countries measures have already been taken in order to reduce the future costs of pensions. Some have decided to extend the contribution period which results in entitlement to a full pension; others are considering increasing the contribution rate, and still others are postponing the indexing of benefits, which decreases their value in real terms. Yet others prefer the solution of introducing a system of notional accounts with defined contributions, which can be considered as a tool which would reduce benefits.

Even though it is quite possible to imagine a combination of different measures implemented in different countries, it can be stated that on the whole all the changes proposed boil down one way or the other to either reducing the benefits or increasing the contributions. Both objectives are achieved by increasing the normal age of retirement. Moreover, this option is favored by many of the countries particularly where the legal ages (men, and women) for entitlement to a pension are relatively low and/or which are facing difficulties regarding a possible increase in the contribution rates. Increasing the retirement age, on condition that people actually work longer, also avoids aggravating the poverty of old people which would result from a simple suppression of benefits. It is also possible that a suppression of benefits may lead to pressures which would oblige pensioners to return to work, either on a full time or on a part time basis. The result would eventually be the same as with raising the legal age of retirement. Thus, either way, future generations will have to work longer.[4]

The issue of resorting to funded systems in order to cope with the problems arising from demographic aging raises the issue of establishing by which method these systems could increase resources thereby eliminating in particular the need of having to reduce pension benefits (see the reasoning provided in the following section). It can be noted here that the Chilean system, often given as an example, did not have the objective, when it was created, of resolving the aging issue, but other types of problems instead.[5]

Defined Contribution Schemes, Return on Investment and Growth

These past few years have been marked in several countries by the increased attention given to the potential effects of the adoption by governments of compulsory defined contribution and fully funded schemes, run by the private sector. These schemes could be either new schemes or schemes resulting form the transformation of a traditional public defined benefit scheme, financed by the pay-as-you-go system. For these new funded pension schemes the advantages which have often been cited mainly consist in a higher average return on investment of retirement savings, less micro-economic distortions, a greater transparency, as well as a potentially positive effect on macro-economic investment and on growth.

The fundamental appeal, for individuals, of the fully funded defined contribution schemes, is the notion that worker contributions are considered as their individual savings, that the investment of theses savings in the capital markets creates relatively high real returns on investment, that the contributions exercise a certain level of control over the choice of the investment portfolio of their assets, and that the uncertainty linked to political risks which can constitute a threat to the benefits provided by schemes operating under the pay-as-you-go system have been eliminated.

Nevertheless, more and more analysts who take an interest in these issues observe that fully funded defined contribution schemes also involve risks and additional costs. In particular, it has been noted through the experience of some countries that there are higher administrative costs linked to the management and running of private pension funds. In addition to this, there exists a risk that in actual fact the accumulated pension assets of the pensioner could finally be significantly less than what had been expected, meaning an amount which could be inferior to the notional value of a flow of defined benefits converted to current value at the moment of retirement. The risk concerning the rate of return on investment can be linked to the quality of the investment strategy implemented by the pension fund or the way in which the government influences this strategy. Alternatively, it could be a systematic risk which applies to all investors as a category. Another important risk is the one linked to the cost required for the markets to provide a sustained offer of return on investment protected against inflation for all the participants, including pensioners (Heller, 1998).

Taking these risks into account as well as the fact that fully funded defined contribution schemes do not allow intergenerational redistribution, nor the implementation of any kind of security net, leads to the reasoning that the approaches leaning towards the implementation of such measures should consider them as supplementary to the defined benefit public schemes, and not as a pillar of dominant public pensions.

At the macroeconomic level, the promoters of the private fully funded pension systems claim that the pension systems operating under the pay-as-you-go method have a negative impact on savings, and that the development of private pension funds should encourage an increase in the global volume of savings, of investments and of their productivity. However, these opinions are far from unanimous.

Without discussing the details of different studies undertaken on this theme, it can be said that the importance and the direction of the impact the two pension systems have on savings and growth still remain the subject of intense debates which economic theory cannot resolve as yet. Given an initial supply of income, an increase in savings cannot be obtained without a decrease in consumption but can be obtained by different ways, which a priori do not necessarily call for the privatization of all or part of the pension systems. One can imagine for example the decrease in the benefit amounts provided by public schemes, or even an increase in taxes. The possibilities of investing, in a manner providing a sustained return and the savings thus obtained give rise to another debate, a few elements of which have just been described above. The difficulty of finding clear answers in economic theory naturally leads participants in theses debates to resort to empirical studies, which in turn provide results which have not been very significant until now, or have even been contradictory on some occasions. The origin of this dead end lies in the difficulty of gathering reliable and comparable data, of specifying the appropriate analytical models of each case, not to mention the differences between econometric estimation techniques used by different authors.

It can be noted that often, in addition to the difficulty of finding a solid theoretical foundation or of being able to rely on significant and conclusive statistical results, the advocates of a transition to fully funded defined contribution schemes forget to take into account the cost of conversion and the different kinds of problems such a change brings about. The basis of the reasoning favoring this change therefore often appears to be ideological.

Conclusion

One can state that to some extent, all societies with a long tradition of social security are in agreement that governments should be involved in the organization of retirement systems. There is a divergence on the issue of the forms that this government involvement should take. Some analysts plead for radically replacing public pay-as-you-go schemes by private measures within a framework where the government's role would be limited to regulating and to guaranteeing a minimum pension. others call for changes which do not involve the replacement of existing pension schemes, but argue for an extension of coverage to more workers in the countries where coverage is not yet universal. There are also the numerous possibilities of multi pillar systems. A question arises concerning all these approaches, namely, of finding out between redistribution objectives and economic efficacy, which type of balance will become dominant in the future, in the temporal management of pension systems.

Higher life expectancy observed in almost all countries has made raising the legal age of retirement appear, for many observers, to be a natural response to the problem of financial balance which demographic aging will certainly create for many pension schemes. What solution should be suggested, with the aim of improving the well being of old persons, between leisure and the need to sue part of the higher life expectancy by working longer, in order to maintain a relatively high level of income upon retirement?

For many sub-Saharan African countries, the issue of the financial viability of pension schemes has been exacerbated by the implementation of structural adjustment measures. As observed by the African chief executive officers of social security institutions who met at Arusha in Tanzania (ISSA, 1994), in most instances these measures did not produce the expected results in areas such as boosting investment, employment, growth, and the well being of the populations. On the contrary, by favoring the suppression of jobs and the closing down of enterprises in the public and private sectors, they have led to an important reduction in the volume of salaries and contributions. What priorities should be favoured in order to introduce a reform which would redress and develop the social security systems of these countries, which were already suffering from slow development compared to other countries (social security coverage of a very limited proportion of the population, staff with limited skills, rate or non-existent actuarial analyses, etc.)?

Many empirical studies suggest that the choice of a pension system (Private or public, under defined contributions or defined benefits) has very little impact on savings, investment, or growth, while in turn this choice can significantly change the distribution of income and of wealth. Following this observation, one is led to the conclusion that passing from one system to the other will inevitably produce winners and losers, and that it is up to those responsible for the reforms to analyse the implications beforehand, and to establish which categories of the population will incur losses, and which ones will obtain profits, and for how long.

Notes

1. See the report of Kalisch and Aman (1997) on this subject.
2. In some countries the reference age selected for the calculation of the rate of old age dependency is 60 years instead of 65 years.
3. It is known in fact that many people among those aged 15 to 64 years do not work (in the traditional economic sense) and therefore do not contribute to the social security pension scheme, and also that a certain number of persons aged 65 years or more do work. The dependency rate defined as the relation between the populations of the age categories defined above is only an approximation of the real dependency rate which would be more complicated to calculate, the level of which would depend on factors such as the time spent in the educational system, the rate of unemployment, the number of persons taking up early retirement, etc.
4. Given a structure with four sources of income: 1. Public pension; 2. Pension stemming from employer measures; 3. Private savings: 4. Income from part time employment) the rcasoning above give a grater role to the fourth type of income in this structure, meaning income derived from part time employment.
5. The Chilean experience, where the advantages and disadvantages have been the subject of a certain number of in-depth analyses, seems to have considerably benefited during its launching from a psychological effect triggered off by the desire to overcome the problems which existed at that point in time (Jollans, 1997).

References

Devereux, S. (1998), Pension system reforms in response to ageing populations, 1996-1998. Draft, ISSA, Geneva.

Heller, P.S. (1998), Rethinking public pension reform initiatives, Working paper, IMP WP/98/61, Washington, D.C.

ISSA (1994), The impact of structural adjustment programmes on social security in African countries, African Series, Social Security Documentation, No.15, Geneva.

ISSA (1995), Pensions de retraite en Afrique Francophone, Serie africaine, documentation de securite sociale, No. 16, Geneva.

Jollans.A. (1997), Pensions and the ageing population, report presented at Staple Innn Actuarial Society, London, 14 October.

Kalish.D. and Aman.T. (1997), Retirement income systems: The reform process across OECD Countries, report presented at the Joint ILO-OECD Workshop: Development and reform of pension sechemes, Paris, 15-17 December.

McGilllivray, W.R. (1997), Pension reforms Tenth Meeting of Heads of ISSA Member Organizations in the English speaking Carribean, Barbados, 26-28 May.

Michaelis, K. (1998), New patterns of sharing responsibilities in the field of social protection: A challenge to social security report presented at the Second Technical Conference of the ISSA, Naples, 25-27 March.

Sorensen. O.B. (1997), Variability of retirement age practices, An appropriate response to the labor market developments, report presented at the First Technical conference of the ISSA, Geneva, 20-27 October.

Thompson.L.H. (1998), Older and Wiser: the Economics of Public pensions, The Urban Institute Press, Washington. D.C.

5

Social Security for the Elderly in Asia and the Pacific

HECTOR INDUCTIVO

The prospect of old age, along with disability and death, has always been the source of constant fear among the most vulnerable members of society. Most countries in the earliest stages of developing their social security schemes have therefore given priority to the provision of protection against these contingencies.

It used to be that in times of economic adversity, the great majority of the people, those living in rural areas, could rely on family and community support. With modernization, urbanization and migration, however, these traditional support arrangements have been greatly eroded, thus exposing a vast number of people, including the elderly population, to the real threat of poverty and deprivation.

Moreover, future prospects are not comforting. In Asia and the Pacific, the population is not only fast growing; it is also fast ageing. According to a World Bank report, of the total population of the world in 1990, 9 per cent or half a billion people were over 60 years old. This number is expected to triple to 1.4 billion by year 2030 and most growth will take place in the developing countries—over half of it in Asia and the Pacific (World Bank, 1992). It has likewise been observed that the rapid pace of ageing in some parts of the region stands in stark contrast to some developed countries. For example, from year 2000, certain developing countries will take only about 25 years or even less to double the proportion of their population aged 65 years and over, i.e., from 7 per cent to 14 per cent (China, Republic of Korea, Thailand and Singapore), compared to such developed countries as Sweden and France, which took 85 and 115 years, respectively, to experience this same increase in the proportion of their elderly population (Perez, 1997; Kinsella, 1995). In fact, in Japan, the ratio of the population over 65 years old has already reached 14.5

Director, Regional Office for Asia and the Pacific International Social Security Asociation.

per cent as of 1995 and is projected to increase further to 25.8 per cent by year 2025 (Ashikaga, 1997).

Furthermore, life expectancy at age 60 years is increasing with the women outliving men in the range of three to five years. This difference in average longevity means that older women greatly outnumber older men; hence, the social, economic and health problems of older populations are in a large part the problems of older women (Kinsella, 1995).

In this scenario, countries in the Asia-Pacific region are increasingly being challenged to provide adequate social protection to their burgeoning elderly populations.

While old-age protection has existed in a few developed countries in the region, since the beginning of the 20th century, notably Australia and New Zealand, the developing countries started addressing the risk of old age only after the Second World War when they established their social security systems.

This paper will discuss the various types of social security schemes and how they have gradually developed to address the needs of the elderly group of the covered populations in the region. It will also present some options that would lead to the enhancement of social security protection for the elderly.

Types of Social Security Schemes in the Region

In Asia and the Pacific, there are three types of social security schemes which have been established to provide protection against the risk of old age, among other social contingencies:

- Social assistance schemes.
- Social insurance schemes.
- Provident fund schemes.

Social Assistance Schemes

Social assistance is a non-contributory scheme which provides social security benefits to all residents and is entirely financed from general revenues of the government. The benefits are either means-tested or universal. Means-tested benefits are determined by the need of the recipients while universal benefits are flat-rate amounts granted to all qualified recipients.

The social assistance approach was pioneered by New Zealand

as far back as 1898, followed by Australia in 1908, starting with the provision of old-age pension benefits. After the war, this type of scheme was also adopted in Brunei Darussalam and Hongkong, China.

Social Insurance Schemes

Social insurance is a compulsory insurance scheme which provides social security benefits to the insured persons and is financed by contributions paid by them or their employers, usually by both, and sometimes with government contributions or subsidies. As with contributions, benefits are earnings-related and usually given in the form of periodic payments although in some rare cases, they are paid in lump sum.

In the Asia and Pacific region, the majority of countries implement social insurance schemes. To a large extent, the development of social insurance as an approach in the provision of social protection has been influenced by ILO through its technical assistance programmes following the adoption of ILO Convention No. 102 in 1952, which embodied the concept of social security based on social insurance principles (McKinnon, Charlton and Munro, 1997).

Provident Fund Schemes

Provident funds are compulsory savings schemes requiring contributions, usually from both the employees and their employers, which are then accumulated into the individual account of the employees. The total accumulated savings, plus interest, are paid in lump-sum to the employee upon his or her retirement.

Most of the countries in Asia which opted for the provident fund approach were former British colonies, although in the case of Pakistan, despite its strong British connection, it decided to establish a social insurance scheme. This is likewise true for many island countries in the Pacific which implement provident fund schemes, although all those that came under the American influence introduced the social insurance approach.

Protection Against the Risk of Old Age: The Asia-Pacific Experience

Coverage

Social security protection of the elderly populations in the region varies depending on the extent of coverage of the schemes in their respective countries.

Under social assistance schemes, all residents are covered and therefore old-age pension benefits are available to all persons who satisfy the prescribed eligibility requirements. It will be noted however that social assistance programmes are costly to implement and therefore available only in the developed countries in the region, including the oil-rich country of Brunei Darussalam.

It is interesting to note that the most developed country in the region, Japan, did not adopt the social assistance approach but instead opted to establish a social insurance scheme that would provide old-age protection for the entire population (Ashikaga, 1997).

The picture is quite different in the countries implementing social insurance and provident fund schemes. In the developing countries, these two programmes were initially designed to cover only the workers in the formal sector. Workers such as those in the informal sector, those in casual or temporary employment, the domestic helpers and the self-employed persons, including those working in establishments with less than a specified number of workers, were excluded from coverage mainly because of the perceived administrative difficulties in identifying them and in enforcing compliance. However, it was the traditional belief that as a consequence of economic growth, most workers would sooner or later enter formal sector employment and hence be covered by the schemes. But as experience has shown, this expectation has not so far materialized; on the contrary and especially in the light of the recent adverse economic developments in the region, an increasing number of workers continue to join the ever expanding informal sector.

In an effort to provide social security protection to these excluded groups of workers, a number of developing countries have extended to some of them either compulsory (Marshall Islands, Micronesia, Palau, Philippines) or voluntary coverage (Bahrain, Malaysia) of the existing schemes. However, the experience of many of these countries has been far from encouraging because of low compliance. A few others have set up special systems for some of this excluded group (Kuwait, Republic of Korea).

Even for workers in the formal sector, widespread evasion has been noted in most developing countries in the region. While it has been frequently mentioned that it is the employees themselves who are resisting their coverage, experience shows that, in most instances, it is mainly the employers, especially the smaller ones, who fail or refuse to comply with the law, either to maximize profits or minimize losses and employees are dissuaded from complaining for fear of dismissal.

In this situation, coverage is low in much of Asia according to the ILO (ILO, 2000) citing for example the scanty coverage of 8 percent of the labour force in India, 10 percent in Thailand (prior to the scheme's expansion in 1995) and 12 percent in Indonesia. Unless coverage is gradually expanded to embrace the excluded sectors of society and effective enforcement machineries are put in place, it is to be expected that the great majority of the elderly populations in the region will face a bleak future, without any significant income support.

Financing Old-age Benefits

As earlier stated, social assistance schemes are funded from government tax revenues. On the other hand, social insurance and provident fund schemes are usually financed by both the employees and their employers although there are some unique instances where only the employees (Afghanistan) or the employers (Pakistan) are required to contribute to the scheme.

Where contributions are required, the rates are based on earnings, with the employers usually paying a higher rate than the employees (Indonesia, Iran, Jordan, Philippines, Turkey), although in a number of schemes, the contributions are shared equally between the employers and employees (Kiribati, Nepal). The government rarely contributes to these schemes and if it does, the contribution is minimal as in the case of India, although in Japan, it finances a third of the first tier national pension scheme.

Old-age Benefit

Under social assistance and social insurance schemes, old-age benefit is usually paid in the form of a pension although there are a few instances of social insurance schemes where the benefit is paid in lump sum (Taiwan, Lebanon).

Under the social insurance schemes, the amount is determined by a formula specified in the law while under social assistance schemes, it is either flat-rate or means-tested. In both cases, the pension benefit is usually paid to the retirees for life. Under social insurance schemes, the pension amounts are usually increased by an increment for those with contributions in excess of the minimum contributory requirement (Kuwait, Philippines).

On the other hand, provident fund schemes pay the benefit in a lump sum, representing the accumulated contributions credited to the account of the individual employees, plus interest. However, a number of countries operating provident fund schemes have since incorporated some pension features into their schemes. In India, part of the employers' share and the full government contribution are diverted to fund an employee pension scheme. Nepal provides for the payment of a pension for a limited period upon retirement without any extra financial liability on the part of either the employers or the employees. Fiji has also introduced a feature in its provident fund scheme which gives the members or their survivors the option to receive a monthly pension, in lieu of the lump sum benefit. In Singapore, members of the Central Provident Fund are required to set aside upon retirement at age 55 a minimum sum in a retirement account to finance a regular monthly benefit after age 62.

Qualifying Conditions

For entitlement to retirement benefits, certain basic requirements have to be satisfied.

Age requirement: Countries in the region differ in regard to the age at which a person may qualify for retirement benefit. The usual retirement age is 60 years under social insurance schemes and 55 years under provident fund schemes.

Obviously, the higher retirement age under social insurance is necessitated by financial considerations in as much as the benefit is payable as lifetime pension and a lower retirement age would result in increased cost to the scheme, especially considering the increasing life expectancy of persons at age 60. On the other hand, the entire benefit under the provident fund is paid in lump sum to the retiree after which all financial obligations on the part of the scheme are thereby terminated.

There are also some countries that set different retirement ages for men and women but this is generally true only for those implementing social insurance schemes. In such cases, the usual retirement age is 60 for men and 55 for women, the assumption being that men would naturally work longer than women (Drouin and Woodall, 1999). In some schemes, retirement at an earlier age, usually not more than five years below the normal retirement age, is allowed for those engaged in arduous or hazardous work (China, Iran, Vietnam, former USSR republics).

Even if the required pensionable age has not been reached, a number of schemes also allow receipt of the regular pension (Iraq, Japan, Syria) or reduced pension (Bahrain, Oman) if contributions have been paid for a longer period than what is required for those retiring at the normal pensionable age.

Period of Contributions/Residence Requirement: Under social insurance schemes, the minimum number of contributions required ranges from ten to 25 years. Where the required number of contributions have not been paid, a few schemes allow the receipt of a reduced pension (Korea) or lump sum benefit (Cyprus, Iraq, Philippines) although some schemes allow the worker to voluntarily continue paying contributions even after reaching retirement age in order to complete the minimum number required for pension benefit (Jordan, Philippines).

In most schemes having a different retirement age for men and women, the period of contributions required for men is higher, usually by five years, than for women (Oman, former USSR republics).

With respect to non-contributory social assistance schemes, a certain period of residence is required for entitlement to pension benefit. Australia requires ten years of continuous residence or five continuous years if the period of residence exceeds ten years; on the other hand, New Zealand requires ten years of residence, of which five should have been spent in the country since the age of 50. Hongkong, China requires five years of continuous residence.

In the case of provident fund schemes, however, the very nature of the benefits, which is merely a refund of accumulated contributions, plus interest, does not require payment of a minimum number of contributions.

Retirement from Employment Requirement: Under social insurance schemes, retirement from employment is usually required for the payment of normal pension benefit. However, there are schemes where retirement or separation from work is not necessary (Pakistan), although in some cases the amount of pension is reduced if the retiree remains in employment (Israel, Korea). There are also instances when retirement from employment is not required after reaching a certain age higher than the normal retirement age (Philippines).

On the other hand, for provident funds, retirement from

employment is not usually required although there are a number of schemes where this is necessary (Kiribati, Nepal, Papua New Guinea, Sri Lanka).

Earnings/means-testing Requirement: Earnings and means-testing are usually applied under the non-contributory social assistance programmes to determine entitlement to pension benefits. The application of such tests could limit the amount of the pension or even result in the denial of the same, depending on the level of earnings from employment or income from other sources.

Measures Taken to Address the Increasing Cost of Social Security

Long-term financial stability is critical to social security schemes. Pension benefits to the elderly account for a significant share in the overall social security expenditures. Given the trend of population ageing in the region and the increasing cost of social security, certain corrective measures have been adopted by a number of countries to ensure the continuing sustainability of their social assistance or social insurance schemes. These measures consisted in either raising the retirement age, increasing the contribution rates, raising the ceiling of covered wages, reducing benefits or applying more restrictive means tests.

In Australia, for example, the pensionable age for women was gradually raised starting July 1995, from age 60 at the rate of 6 months every two years until it reaches age 65 which is the qualifying age for men. In Japan, the retirement age under the Employees' Pension Insurance will gradually be increased from 60 to 65 years of age in year 2013 for males and 2018 for females. The pensionable age of 62 years under the New Zealand Superannuation will also rise progressively until it reaches age 65 by the year 2001. In Kuwait, the retirement age will be gradually increased from age 50 to 55 by year 2020. In the Republic of Korea, the pensionable age will be raised from 60 to 65 years by year 2033.

Likewise in Australia, some means tests have been made more stringent. For instance, income tests applying for Family Payments were extended to include income from overseas while amounts deducted from taxable income tests due to negative gearing of rental properties will now be added to the Family Payment income test. While making the Mature Age Allowance a permanent feature of the allowance system, its payment was made subject to an income and assets test and the 'no recent workforce experience' requirement.

Another approach adopted by some countries to meet the rising cost of the pension schemes is to increase the contribution rate or the ceiling of wages subject to contributions. For example, in the Marshall Islands, the contributions made by employers and employees were increased by 1 percent each raising the total contributions to 12 percent, while in the Republic of Korea, the contribution rate of 3 percent of earnings is scheduled to be raised to 9 per cent for the self-employed, farmers, fishermen and the voluntarily insured persons by year 2005. In Japan, contributions to both the National Pension and the Employees' Pension Schemes will gradually increase from the present 17.35 percent to a maximum of 30 per cent by year 2025. In India, the employee and employer contributions to the Provident Fund have recently been increased from 10 to 12 per cent. On the other hand, the present wage ceilings have been increased in Pakistan and the Philippines.

The Road to the Future

From the historical development of social security and recent trends in the Asia and Pacific region, certain lessons may be drawn that would help formulate the vision of what it should be in the years to come to ensure adequate social security protection for the elderly populations. The diversity in the level of development among the different countries and the demographic transformation that is emerging in the region have earlier been noted. These countries must endeavor to ensure that the fruits of economic growth are shared by the lowest strata of the population on the basis of equity and social justice principles. Social security plays a vital role in the accomplishment of this goal. Thus, countries in the region must take a hard look at their existing schemes and try to adopt innovative measures and arrangements that would enable them to be equal to the rising demands of the future.

1. Towards Comprehensive Coverage: As earlier observed, social security protection continues to elude a vast majority of the region's populations: the rural workers, the self-employed persons, the workers in casual or informal employment and other low-income workers. The countries in the region must take the necessary steps to bring them under the aegis of social security.

2. Towards Social Assistance for All: In most countries, governments have shifted a significant part of the responsibility of providing social protection for the people to the people themselves, either through contributory social insurance or provident fund savings schemes. The limited coverage of these schemes, however, prevents a large number of the populations from enjoying social protection. Somehow, all countries must gear towards providing a safety net for their entire populations through the mechanism of social assistance and not just through whatever public services and other arrangements are made available under state budgets.

3. Towards a Pension Scheme: Lump-sum benefits payable under provident funds have always been regarded as inadequate in providing long-term security for the elderly, the disabled and the dependent survivors of deceased workers. Lump-sum benefits may provide huge amounts of money to the recipients upon their retirement but such amounts could easily be dissipated if unwisely spent or invested, thus leaving them in penury for the rest of their lives.

A substantial part of the contributions of provident fund members may be set aside to finance the payment of lifetime pension benefits.

4. Towards a Uniform Pensionable Age: In many countries, the pensionable age for men is higher, usually by five years, than that for women. This raises the issue of equity, especially if the longer life span of women is considered. This means more contributions and shorter entitlement for men and less contributions and longer entitlement for women. Such a difference might have been acceptable when there were relatively few working women but not anymore in the light of increasing women's participation in the labour market. This situation therefore needs to be corrected by providing a uniform pensionable age for both men and women. By raising the pensionable age for women to the level of that for men, fairness and equity will be served; furthermore, it will help improve the financial status of the schemes.

5. Towards the Protection of Migrant Workers: With the globalization of the economy, migration has been the answer to the shortage of labour in many countries throughout the world. Yet, there are a number of these countries that do not extend social security protection to migrant workers. National social security systems should therefore be made to cover these foreign workers for after all, they contribute significantly to the economic development of their countries of employment.

But even where migrant workers are covered by the social security schemes of the countries where they are employed, their protection may be lost when they move on to other countries. There is therefore a need to coordinate the social security schemes of the various countries that would, for instance, enable the tacking of the periods of coverage under the different schemes for entitlement to the pension benefits provided under them. Moreover, once entitled to the benefit, they should be allowed to receive the benefit regardless of where they reside.

These measures should be made possible through bilateral or multilateral social security agreements among countries.

6. Towards Meaningful Social Security Benefits: In most pension schemes, no provision is made for the indexation or automatic adjustment of benefits to compensate for the eroding effects of inflation. Without indexation or adjustment of the pension benefits, their real value will gradually drop and the protection they provide will ultimately become illusory. Of course there are schemes which allow adhoc adjustments but they may not be sufficient to protect the real value of the benefits. It may be well for countries to incorporate a provision in the scheme for the indexation or automatic adjustment of pension benefits.

7. Towards Better Investment of Social Security Funds: Contributions to social security should be used for the exclusive benefit of the contributors. This means that social security funds should be invested with due diligence and prudence to earn the highest possible rate of interest consistent with safety so that through the earnings the benefits may be improved. It is a common practice for government to access social security funds through the issuance of government securities and bonds earning interest at below market rates. If governments have to utilize these funds to finance their projects, they should at least give these funds a fair return on investment. Furthermore, government policies regulate the investment of social security funds which often prevent their placement in better and higher yielding investments. These policies must be liberalized and where there is a dearth of local investment opportunities, investment abroad should be allowed.

8. Towards Better Services for Members: Social security systems can only be effective if benefits are paid to the right person in the right amount and at the right time and place. In this age of modern and sophisticated technology, social security institutions must decentralize with full computer support to fulfill this basic mandate. All manual operations, to the extent possible, must be automated for speedier action. Records must be properly maintained for easy retrieval whenever needed.

But most of all, social security institutions must be staffed by dedicated and competent men and women who are totally committed to serve their members.

References

Ashikaga, Shoji, 1997, The national experience of Japan, in *Asia and the Pacific Series No. 23: Social Security in Asia and the Pacific* (Manila, ISSA Regional Office for Asia and the Pacific), pp. 215-225.

Beattie, Roger, 1998, Pension systems and prospects in Asia and the Pacific, in *International Social Security Review* (Geneva, ISSA), Vol. 51, No. 3, pp. 63-87.

Drouin, Anne and Woodall, John, 1999, Pensionable age in Asia: Trends and Implications, in *Asia and Pacific Series No. 25: Social Security Challenges in Asia and the Pacific* (Manila, ISSA Regional Office for Asia and the Pacific), pp. 111-140.

International Labour Office, 2000, *Social Security Pensions, Development and Reform* (International Labour Office, Geneva).

Kinsella, Kevin, 1995, *Population Ageing in Developing Countries*, paper presented at the Experts' Group Meeting organized by the International Institute on Ageing (UN Malta) in collaboration with the United Nations Population Fund in Malta in October 1995.

McKinnon, Roddy, Charlton, Roger and Munro, Harry, T., 1997, The national provident fund model: An analytical and evaluative reassessment, in *International Social Security Review*, (Geneva, ISSA), Vol. 50, No. 2, pp. 43-61.

Perez, Aurora, E., 1997, Implications of demographic trends in Asia and the Pacific, in *Asia and Pacific Series No. 23: Social Security in Asia and the Pacific* (Manila, ISSA Regional Office for Asia and the Pacific), pp. 45.

U.S. Social Security Administration, 1999. *Social Security Programs Throughout the World-1999*, (Washington, DC).

World Bank, 1994. *Averting the old age crisis: Policies to protect the old and promote growth* (Oxford University Press, New York).

6

Elderly in Asian Countries and Social Security

R. K. A. SUBRAHMANYA

The arrangements for providing social security to the elderly in Asian countries are extremely diverse. In some countries there is practically no provision for social security for the elderly while in some other countries the entire population is covered under highly sophisticated arrangements. In between these extremes there are countries where provident fund or pension provisions exist for selected groups of people. This diversity is exemplified in this chapter.

I. BANGLADESH

In Bangladesh, traditionally, the responsibility for the welfare of the elderly lies with their children and the State has virtually no obligation to provide for the elderly. Culture demands that a son, preferably the eldest son, should look after his parents in their oldage. This system therefore provides that elderly persons should co-reside with their sons. Daughters are considered to be temporary guests in the family. They are married off when they reach the appropriate age. According to prevailing social norms, even if a daughter wants, she is not expected to directly look after her parents or have her parents live with her.

The traditional system of inter-generational co-residence is said to be widespread in Bangladesh. Bangladesh gives evidence that the majority of elderly people continue to live within extended family settings both in rural and urban areas, though there may be variations by sex, area of residence and the socio-economic situation of the elderly and social changes have not eroded the significance of the joint family.

It is said that the kind of social security system that exists for the elderly in many high income countries is not a viable option for Bangladesh in the foreseeable future. With large sections of other population groups drawing upon the already constrained financial resources of the country, the elderly are not perceived to be a priority group for government support.

The Constitution of Bangladesh, however, provides that the needy elderly people have a right to social security. In the fourth Five Year Plan (1990-95) the first financial allocation of Taka 5 million was made for the welfare of the elderly under the jurisdiction of the Ministry of Social Welfare. A National Committee of Aging was formed at the government level to look after the welfare of the elderly.

Old-age Homes

Provision was also made for setting up six oldage homes called "Shanti Nibash". for old people in need of social support. Under the programme poor elderly persons of more than 60 years of age with none to take care of them will be admitted to the "Shanty Nibash" with greater priority to women in the ratio of forty male and 60 female They will be provided shelter, clothing, food, medical treatment including medicines free of cost. The aged people having no kith and kin will be buried after death at the cost of the "Shanti Nibash". There will be a management committee for each Nibash to look after the admission and day to day management of the homes.

Depending on the physical conditions and ability of the persons they will be given training to enable them to be engaged in gainful activities. There will also be facilities for recreation for the elderly housed in the Homes.[1] One such home has been set up so far.[2]

Old-age Pension

In April 1997 the then Government of Bangladesh introduced for the first time a scheme for payment of an allowance to the needy elderly called Boyosko Bhata (Elderly Allowance).

Under this scheme the ten poorest and oldest persons are paid an allowance of 100 taka each (US$ 2) in each ward (administrative unit) throughout the country Of these not less than 50 per cent of the beneficiaries are to be women. The selection of beneficiaries is done according to well defined criteria involving age, economic conditions, and health status. Those who are aged, sick or disabled have no land and have an annual income of less than 3000 taka are classified as destitute and receive priority There are at present over 400, 000 beneficiaries under the scheme The scheme is implemented in partnership with the members of the civil society.[3]

Government Employees

In Bangladesh Government employees of all levels enjoy pension gratuity and other benefits after their retirement.

2. CHINA

Transition from Family Support to Social Security

China is gradually transforming the system of social protection of the elderly from family care to social security. Considering the characteristics of the "dual economy" existing in the country and the state of unbalanced regional development, China has selected, over a longer period of time, a multi-tiered old-age security system separately managed to protect the aged in the urban and rural areas.

The Multi-tiered System

There are broadly three main kinds of pension schemes in China, the pension scheme for civil servants and employees of public institutions, the voluntary rural pension scheme and the basic pension scheme for urban workers.

In the urban area, the public pension insurance of the enterprise employees is administered by the governments at different levels. Besides the formal old-age insurance for salary and waged workers, the means-tested benefits are also provided as minimum living protection for the elderly without any source of income.

In the rural areas, the individual accumulated savings system mainly provides the basic old-age protection with family support supplemented by social assistance schemes.

Pension scheme for civil servants and employees of public institutions

The budget financed pension scheme for civil servants and employees of public institutions covers nearly 30 million people. Military personnel have a similar but independent pension scheme. The rate of pension is determined on the basis of the individual's salary and the period of service rendered by him. In recent years, there is a move to reduce the liability of the government by covering certain categories of such employees under the basic pension scheme for urban workers.

The Basic Pension Scheme for Urban Workers

The basic pension scheme for urban workers, which combines social pooling with individual account, is based on the 1986 State Council Decision on establishing a Unified Basic Oldage Insurance System for enterprise workers. It covers all kinds of enterprises with foreign investment, Chinese urban enterprises and public institutions managed as enterprises (as well as self employed workers in certain places at the discretion of each provincial government). The scheme covered around 106 million people i.e., 90 per cent of the targeted population, in 2001.

The basic pension fund is pooled at the provincial level and the contribution rate varies from one province to another. In May 2001, the nationwide average pension contribution rate reached 22 per cent of payroll for employers and 5 per cent for employees.

An individual account equivalent to 11 per cent of payroll is established for each worker. It is composed of the total individual contribution and a supplement from the employers contribution. The rest of the employers contribution, an average of 16 percent, goes into the local pooling fund.

Upon reaching retirement age, which is 60 for male and 50 for females worker an employee with at least 15 years of contribution is entitled to a two component pension. The first component is the universal flat rate benefit, which is fixed at 20 percent of the regional average wage of the previous year and disbursed from the pooling fund. The second is the individual account pension benefit which is 1/120 of the accumulation in the employee's individual account. The target replacement rate for a retiree with 35 years of contribution is 58.5 per cent.

The individual account pension is paid to the retiree throughout his or her lifetime although theoretically the account's accumulation is only sufficient for ten years' payment. If the retiree dies within ten years any remaining balance in the account can be transferred to his or her beneficiary.[4]

Rural Pension Scheme

The rural pension scheme, which was introduced in 1991, is a voluntary scheme based on contributions by the individuals living in rural areas, supplemented by a collective subsidy. An individual account is established for each participant to which his contributions are credited. The individual will be entitled to a benefit based on the accumulation in the account on attaining the age of 60. From 2001, after ten years from the date of introduction, the scheme covers around 61.69 million rural people from more than 200 counties. The total amount accumulated in the rural pension fund was 19.55 billion yuans. The scheme is administered by county level rural social insurance organisations. There is currently a move to privatize the scheme.[5]

Community-based Care Services

Income security through pension schemes is supplemented by community based services for taking care of the elderly.

The community care policies were first launched in the 1980s. Since then, through the efforts by the local community and government action, nearly one million community care establishments, over 5,000 community service centers and over one million residents convenience stations have been set up all over the country. 85 per cent of these facilities provide service to the elderly. The main programs of the community care system are as follows:

(a) Daily care services: including feeding, haircutting, housework, shopping and assistance in communicating with family members; repair of household appliances, tailoring, etc.,

(b) Health care including medical care, physical check-up, emergency service, rehabilitation service; home consulting, mobile out-patient service, provision of family hospital beds, mutual cooperative health program in rural areas etc.;

(c) Cultural activities: including entertainment including fashion show, dancing, TV supply of newspapers, games like chess and cards; life-long learning program with 13, 000 Old-age Universities teaching English language, computer, history, family education, calligraphy, painting and cooking courses (there are presently more than one million elderly students undergoing these courses); and

(d) Re-employment: Providing job development, job counselling and job placement to help the younger elderly more employable.[6]

Legislative Development

Since the 1950s, a series of laws have been enacted for the protection of the elderly. In August 1996, the Law of Protecting the Rights of the Elderly of the People's Republic of China was enacted. This Law defines the rights of the elderly and provides that the families are mainly responsible for the care of the elderly and that the members of the family should perform the duties to take care of the older persons in their families.

3. INDONESIA

In Indonesia, oldage disability and survivor benefits are provided in three ways—Government employees are entitled to pension and the employees in the private sector are covered partly under a provident fund scheme and partly under private pension schemes.

Public Sector

The Government Civilian Employees are entitled to theses benefits under the Savings and Insurance Scheme. The scheme provides for

(1) pensions calculated on the final monthly salary at the rate of 2.5 per cent of basic salary per year of service;
(2) lump sum payments of 16.5 months salary on retirement or earlier death;
(3) On death of the employee, before or after retirement, a monthly pension is paid to the widow or widower (or to the children if there is no spouse).

Pensions are adjusted to the variations in the Consumer Price Index at the same time and on the same basis as the earnings of employees still in service.

The employees contribute a total of 8 per cent of earnings (4.75 per cent for pensions and 3.25 per cent for lump sum payments) for these benefits.

Expenditure on lump sum benefits and the cost of 22.5 per cent of pension benefits are met from the employees contributions and income derived from those contributions. The balance is met by government.

Administration of the scheme is the responsibility of the Ministry of Finance. It is run by an organisation called P T Taspen.

This scheme is building up considerable unfunded liabilities. It has been projected that pensions which account for about 30 percent of the civil service wage bill will increase to 70 per cent by 2020.

Taspen is currently one of the most important investor in the Indonesian financial markets and owns one third of the country's pension assets. It suffered some reverses in the recent financial crisis and is now building up its reserves. The scheme has the following weaknesses:

(i) Labor mobility is inhibited by the limited vesting rights; civil servants who leave before age 50 lose all pension rights including their own contributions.

(ii) Pension is based on the final month's earnings rather than related to a longer period of earnings and this may not reflect normal earnings patterns.

(iii) The pension scheme for the Armed Forces has a structure similar to the civilian scheme.

(iv) Administration of that Scheme is the responsibility of the Ministry of Defense. It is run by PT Asabri.

Private Sector: Provident Fund Scheme

Private sector employees are governed by a provident fund scheme. It is applicable to workers in the formal sector including the employees of State owned enterprises.

The scheme is applicable to all establishment employing 10 or more persons on a monthly payroll of Rupiah 1 million or more.

Under the Scheme employers contribute 3.7 per cent and workers contribute 2 per cent of their earnings. These contributions are credited into individual accounts of the workers.

The accumulations in these accounts are paid back with interest on retirement at age 55 or earlier in the event of invalidity, death, or migration. Members who have at least 5.5 years membership can also withdraw the balance in their account if they become unemployed.

The scheme is administered by PT Jamsostek a public limited company with government owning 100% shares. There is a tripartite board of Commissioners (5 persons) answerable to the Minister of Manpower on technical and policy matters and to the Minister of Finance on financial matters. It is aimed at formal sector workers in the private sector and employees in State owned enterprises.

As at the end of 1998, Jamsostek had registered 14.9 million insured persons and 82544 employers, covering only 50 per cent of the formal sector labor force and 13 per cent of the national labour force. In particular those excluded are those who work for small employers. Approximately 80 per cent of the investible funds are invested in time deposits in banks.

Private Sector: Private Pension Schemes

Law 11.92 on Pension Funds provides a legal and regulatory framework for the development of Employers Pension Funds and Financial Institution Pension funds under the supervision of the Ministry of Finance. By the end of 1997, approximately 1.2 million employees were members of such Funds.

Although private schemes and arrangements based on collective agreements have existed for some years the implementation of the Law11/92 on Pension Funds was a major advance in the development of social protection in the area of pensions. The Act regulates the structure and operation of Employers Pension funds administered by employers through Foundations and Financial Institution Pension Funds operated by commercial insurance companies or banks, All such funds are required to be registered with the Ministry of Finance.

As on 31st December 1997, there were 311 EPFs covering 1.046,869 active members and 44,034 beneficiaries. Of these 242 schemes were defined benefit schemes and they were required to provide pension with an accrual rate per year of service not greater than 2.5 per cent and a maximum replacement rate of 80 per cent of monthly salary.

According to these schemes retirement age is 55 with provision for early retirement between 45 and 55.

Widows and widowers are eligible for pension benefits on the death of an insured person whether before or after retirement.

Members who leave service with less than three years of membership con be refunded their contributions plus interest. If they have more than 3 years of service there is provision for a deferred pension. If separation takes place more than 10 years before retirement pension rights can be transferred to another EPF or FIPF.

Employers contribution to the EPFs are determined by actuarial valuation and employers contributions must be 7.5 per cent of pensionable earnings or three times the accrual rate times of pensionable earnings whichever is the lesser. Contribution are tax deductible while pension benefits are taxable income.

As on 31st December 1997, 24 banks and insurance companies were operating FIPFs in respect of 150,000 active participants. The benefit structure is similar to that of EPFs.

Both EPFs and FIPFs are fully funded and thus play an important role in the Indonesian financial markets in spite of the relatively small number of schemes. Total assets of the EPFs as on 31st Dec 1997 were Rp 15,812 million and of FIFPs 388,000.

About 10 percent of the formal sector labour force is covered by these schemes. It appears that many employers find them unattractive for a variety of reasons. Many employers have only a small labor force with high rate of turnover and view participation in a pension fund as a costly and time consuming burden; particularly when employees are already covered by mandatory public schemes such as Jamostek and by labor legislation for severance payments Among the rules that make pensions unattractive to employers are:

(a) Funding of pension obligations through a separate foundation.
(b) Vesting of pension benefits after a short period of employment.
(c) Low retirement age of 55.
(d) 80 per cent of benefits are paid in the form of an annuity even when the amount is small.
(e) Unfavourable tax treatment.

Private pension funds have become a policy option for Ministry of Financé not only to improve pension protection for employees but also to strengthen the capital markets by ensuring significant growth in the volume of investments by private pension funds.

4. KOREA

There are several public pension schemes in Korea. These are:

(i) The National Pension Scheme.
(ii) The Government Employees Pension Scheme.
(iii) The Military Personnel Pension Scheme.
(iv) Private School Teachers Pension Scheme.
(v) Specially designated Post office Employees Pension Scheme.

National Pension Scheme

The National Pension Scheme, the most important one, was established under the National Welfare Pension Act, 1973 which was later called the National Pension Act in 1988. Initially, the National Pension Scheme was applicable to those working in workplaces with more than 10 full time employees. It was later extended to all workplaces with more than 5 full time employees (1992), farmers and fishermen (July 1995) and urban citizens (April 1999) and eventually to the entire population satisfying the general coverage criteria except those covered under special schemes mentioned above. Foreigners residing in Korea are also covered under the scheme since 1995. The general coverage criteria are age and residence. Income is not a relevant criterion.

The scheme envisages four classes of members. Accordingly, all residents in Korea from 18 to > 60 years, regardless of their income are covered under the scheme. The persons covered under the scheme are classified as follows:

(i) Workplace based insured persons.
(ii) Individually insured persons.
(iii) Voluntarily insured persons (Those who are not subject to mandatory coverage but who are covered on their application).
(iv) Voluntarily and Continuously Insured Persons (The current and former Insured Persons will lose his or her insured status upon reaching the age of 60 but those with less than a 20 year insured period may continue their participation in the Scheme if they apply to do so).

The National Pension Scheme is designed to assure a minimum income regardless of previous income levels. The pension benefit under the scheme is based on the average income of all insured persons. Thus the income replacement rate is set higher than the previous income in some cases while it is set lower than their previous income in other cases. This is done with the object of achieving redistribution of income so that those who were at a high income level help to raise the post-retirement income of those who were at a low income level. The benefit amount in any case is also proportional to the average income over one's total insured period on which his /her contributions are paid.

The income level secured by the scheme is about 60 per cent of average income of an average income earnings with a 40 year insured period. The real value of benefit is maintained by applying consumer price index to benefit amount every year.

The National Pension Scheme is a social insurance scheme. The scheme is financed by contributions from the insured persons and their employers. The contributions of workplace based insured persons are shared equally by the employer and the employees. In the case of individually insured persons including voluntarily insured persons and voluntarily and continuously insured persons the contributions are paid by the respective individuals alone. Government provides financial support temporarily for some portion of contributions payable by farmers and fishermen. The administrative cost of the scheme is also borne partially by the State.

The scheme provides for enhancement of the rates of contributions progressively so that the future generations contribute more than the current generation. This represents the intergenerational redistributive element in the scheme. The rates are revised once every five years. taking into account all relevant factors.

The rate of contribution for work placed insured persons was fixed initially at 3 per cent; it was raised to 6 per cent in 1993 and to 9 per cent in 1998, shared equally by the employer (4.5 per cent) and the employee (4.5 per cent).

The contribution rate for individually insured persons and voluntarily and continuously individually insured persons was 3% from July 1995 to June 2000; it is being enhanced by 1 per cent annually thereafter so that it is expected to reach 9 per cent by July 2005.

In the case of farmers and fishermen the rates of contributions are fixed in a graded manner, there being altogether 45 grades and government's subsidy is limited to one third of the contribution at the lowest grade.

Persons who cannot pay contributions or have difficulty in paying it because of lack of or low income are exempted from paying contributions.

The National Pension Fund is a partially funded system.

It is a defined benefit system providing for gradual increase in the rates of contributions.

It mitigates the burden on the future generations by using profits gained from the fund as benefit expenditure when the scheme matures.

The minimum insurance period for oldage pension is 10 years. Those who do not meet this requirement can extend their insured period and acquire the right to benefit by making contributions on a voluntary basis. In addition the insured persons are given opportunities to convert a period of non-contribution – a period of exceptions of contributions payment or a period for which lumpsum refund is made—to an insured period. These eliminate the possibility of insured persons being unable to acquire a pension right because of insured period.

There is a Special Oldage pension scheme for persons who attain the age of 60 without meeting the minimum insured period requirement. In such cases the minimum insured period for the title to pension is 5 years.

In the case of disability or survivor pension there is no requirement of minimum insured period and pension benefits may be paid in the event of disability or death during ones insured period.

A scheme of divided pension has been introduced to provide income protection to non-income earning spouses, mainly housewives, who are not mandatorily covered under the scheme

There is no age limit for a female spouse for receiving survivor pension benefits.[7]

5. MALAYSIA

As in other countries of Asia, the family is the main bulwark for the welfare of the aged people in Malayasia both in monetary terms and in the provision of social care. At present it is common practice for the aged parents to co-reside with their adult children. Data drawn from the Second Malayasian Family Life Survey (MFLS-2) (1993) indicate that more than two thirds of Malayasians aged over 60 co-reside with their adult children. There are also economic incentives to continue the practice. Adult children who live with their parents enjoy a tax rebate of RM 1000, there is provision for tax deduction up to RM1000 for medical expenses incurred by adult children for the care of elderly parents and a further tax deduction up to RM 1000 for purchase of necessary equipment for disabled persons. However the dual processes of rapid industrialization and urbanization resulting in growing dispersion of people and reduction in family size have had a detrimental effect on the ability of the family to offer support to the elderly people. It has necessitated the development of formal systems of social security.

Employed Provident Fund

The most important sources of non-familial support for the elderly in Malayasia is the Employees Provident Fund (EPF).

EPF plays a central role in the provisions of income security for the elderly in Malayasia. It is a publicly mandated savings plan with contributions shared between employers and employees. It was established under the EPF Act 1951. It is said to be the oldest provident fund in the world.

The scheme is fully funded. The main role of the EPF is to provide financial security to its members after retirement. All employees irrespective of the size of their employer's business, are covered by the scheme. Contributions are made by the employers as well as the employees to the EPF. The current rates of contribution are: 12 per cent by employers and 11 per cent by employees. The contributions of each member is placed in three separate dedicated accounts:

Account No. I: At present 60 per cent of the contributions are deposited in Account I. The amount credited to this account may be withdrawn after the member has attained the age 55 in any of the following ways:

- The entire amount may be withdrawn in one single lump sum.
- The amount may be withdrawn partly lump sum, partly by means of periodical payments.
- The entire amount may be drawn by means of periodical payments.
- The dividend may be drawn periodically leaving the balance in the Account.

Account No.II : 30 per cent of the contributions are deposited in Account II. The amount credited to this account may be withdrawn at any time for the purpose of building a house or the payment of housing loans. The balance in this account, that is total contributions plus compound interest less the amount utilized for housing may be withdrawn at age 50.

Account No. III: The remaining 10 per cent of the contributions is credited to Account No. III. The amount lying in this account may be utilized to meet the costs of defined critical medical treatment.

The total balance in the individual accounts can be withdrawn in the following circumstances:

- On death;
- In the event of incapacitation;
- On emigration; and
- On attaining the age of 55.

Any option to take a phased withdrawal of the balance at age 55 for a term of 5, 10 15 or 20 years is available subject to a minimum balance of RM 12000 and a minimum payment of RM 200 per month.

Supplementary Death and Incapacitation Benefits

In the event of death or incapacity an additional lump sum benefit is payable subject to a minimum of RM 1000 and a maximum of RM 30, 000. The amount payable, in any case, is obtained by application of a formula. It is paid out of the investment income accruing to the Fund.

Coverage

As at the end of 1997 the EPF had 8.3 million members of whom an estimated five million members were active contributors. The coverage represents roughly 55 per cent of the labor force.

Investments

Under the 1991 Act, the EPF can invest its funds in certain approved securities:

- Bank Negara or a licensed bank or financial institution;
- Shares of a public company listed on the Malayasian Stock Exchange;
- Debentures of any public company;
- Bonds mortgage papers etc., within the meaning of the Bills of Exchange Act;
- Investments permitted under the Trustee Act;
- Loans to the Federal or a State government;
- Loans to members of the Fund for purchasing or building a house; and
- Loans and shares of an approved company.

Subject to written permission from the Minister, the fund may be invested in :

- Any bank or financial institution;
- A joint venture or privatization programme;
- Loans to any company or corporation; and
- Any investment outside Malayasia.

The investment is subject to the condition that at least 50 per cent of the annual investments and 70 per cent of the total investments at any time should be in Malayasian Government Securities These percentages may be varied by the Minister.

Interest on the balances in the EPF, which is called dividend, is calculated on a compound basis and is paid annually. The rate of dividend is determined by the EPF Board, subject to approval of the Minister of Finance. Under the Act the dividend cannot be less than 2.5 per cent. The real rate of return, that which has exceeded the increase in the CPI, has consistently been positive.

Administration

The EPF is administered by a tripartite Board. The Board has appointed a committee to oversee investments. The day to day administration of the Fund is the responsibility of the General Manager. The EPF maintains a high degree of efficiency in the management of accounts. Its operative costs amount to less than 3 per cent of total revenue.[8]

6. NEPAL

The concept of social security in Nepal is gradually shifting from the realm of the society to the State. Traditionally, the society including the extended joint family system and the community, had performed the role of the social security providers in Nepal. Women, children, the aged and the disabled people were all taken care of by the kith and kin belonging to the joint family system. People still look to that system as the basic source of social security. But in the process of modernization the country has given up the old tradition without accepting the modern norms of social security. The country is passing through a transitional phase.

The Constitution of Nepal requires the State to pursue such policies as will promote the welfare of the vulnerable groups of people including the aged. The Constitution provides for enactment of special legislation for the welfare of the aged people.

The law relating to Government employees provides for payment of pension to them on their retirement from service, the maximum pension being 50 per cent of the pay last drawn.

In the case of industrial labour there is provision of provident fund. The employers as well as the employees contribute to the provident fund 10 per cent of the wages payable to the workers. They are also entitled to gratuity.

The Government of Nepal has adopted a National Policy for the Aged the salient features of which are as follows:

- Senior citizens will be classified into two categories for purposes of giving them assistance; viz., those who are in the age group of 70-75 and those who are above the age of 75.
- Senior citizens, helpless widows and disabled people will be classified into different categories on the basis of certain economic criteria. Degree of vulnerability will be the basis for coverage under the scheme for payment of the allowance under the social assistance programme.
- All zonal hospitals will have geriatric wards.
- Senior citizens will be treated in all the hospitals and health centres at subsidized rates.
- Efforts will be made to obtain concessions in the fees charged by private institutions for treatment of senior citizens.
- Arrangements will be made to organize mobile health services for the benefit of the aged people.
- Oldage Homes will be established in all regions, keeping in view the welfare of senior citizens. NGOs and private entrepreneurs will be encouraged to set up oldage homes.
- Income generating activities will be promoted to suit the skill, knowledge and aptitude of the senior citizens.
- The experience of the senior citizens will be utilized in all nation building activities to the extent possible.
- Senior citizens will be given concessions in public transport.

In terms of this policy the Government is implementing the following programmes:

A monthly allowance of Rs.150 is being paid to persons who are of the age of 75 or more and a monthly allowance of Rs.100 is being paid to widows of the age of 60 or more.

Government is running an elderly home in Kathmandu with 180 inmates. Government is giving financial assistance to about ten NGOs for establishing and maintaining oldage homes.[9]

7. PAKISTAN

There are sixty eight 'labour laws in Pakistan of which the following laws relate to social security:

1. Employees Oldage Benefits Act, 1976.
2. Provincial Employees Social Security Ordninance 1965.
3. The Workers Welfare Fund Ordinance.
4. The Companies Profits (Workers Participation) Act, 1968.
5. The Excise Duty on Minerals (Labour Welfare) Act, 1967.
6. The Workers children (Education) Ordinance 1972.
7. West Pakistan Standing Orders Ordinance 1968.

The Oldage Benefits Scheme is the main pension scheme for workers. The scheme was launched in 1976 by the enactment of the Employees Oldage Benefit Act, 1976. The object of the scheme is to provide oldage benefits to persons employed in industrial, commercial and other organisations. The benefits include oldage pension, invalidity pension, survivors' pension (widows' pension) and oldage grant. The scheme is applicable to establishments employing 10 or more persons including managerial and administrative personnel. There is a wage limit for application of the scheme. The current limit for contribution and benefits is Rs.3000 p.m. A person once covered remains covered even if his wage exceeds the limit.

The scheme is financed through contribution by the employers and the Government. The rate of contribution by the employers is 5 per cent. Initially the Federal government was also contributing at the same rate. Government contribution has since been discontinued with effect from 1st July 1995. No contribution is payable by the employees. Thus at present only the employer is contributing to the scheme.

Initially, administration of the scheme was entrusted to the State Life Insurance Corporation of Pakistan. In 1981 the administration of the scheme was transferred to an independent tripartite Board of Trustees of which the Secretary, Federal Ministry of Labour is the President. The Scheme provides for the following benefits:

- Oldage Pension.
- Invalidity Pension.
- Survivors Pension.
- Oldage Grant.

Oldage pension is subject to a minimum of Rs.630 per month (with effect from 1st January 2000) and a maximum of Rs. 2400 per month.

As on 30th June 2000, the Board had registered 42,479 employers and 1.52 million employees. The amount of contributions collected was Rs.13,293 million The total number of pensioners was 173,362.

The total amount of pension disbursed up to June 2000 was Rs.6,146 million. The Institution was maintaining a fund of Rs. 41,466 million and an investment portfolio of Rs.32,647 million on which it had earned an income of Rs.5,328 million. It is a life pension scheme. In case of death of the pensioner, including an invalidity pensioner, his pension is passed on to his widow or children. The survivor's pension is 100 per cent of the deceased worker's pension.

If an insured person is not survived by any spouse the survivors pension is paid to the children in equal shares till they attain the age of 18 or until marriage whichever is earlier. If there is no minor child of the deceased pensioner the survivors pension is paid to the surviving parents for five years.

There is provision for payment of survivors pension to the surviving parents of the deceased insured person if any, in case of death of the surviving spouse in receipt of survivors' pension if there are no minor children.

The oldage grant (gratuity) is payable in lump sum equal to one month's average wage for every completed year of insurable employment. The period of employment qualifying for the gratuity is two years. The minimum oldage pension is Rs. 630 per month and the maximum pension is Rs. 2400 per month. The survivors pension is equivalent to 100 per cent of the deceased pensioners pension.

The Scheme is reported to be under review by a high level committee headed by the Deputy Chairman of the Planning Commission of Pakistan. The Committee is said to be examining the following proposals:

(a) Introduction of an Individual Pensions Account system for all employees working in private sector and extension of the Scheme in the form of Defined Contribution (Individual Pension Account) Scheme in a progressive manner to all employees presently not covered and self employed persons.

(b) Extension of the scheme to all establishments employing even one employee.

(c) Coverage of self-employed persons and other workers including agricultural workers.

(d) Enhancement of the wage ceiling to Rs. 5000.

(e) Enhancement of the maximum pension to Rs. 5000.

(f) Indexation of the benefits.

In order to meet the rising cost of the pension scheme it is proposed to raise the rates of contribution.

Eventually, every worker in an industry establishment or other organisation in the formal and informal sector will be covered under the proposed individual pension scheme or the scheme under the EOBI Act, 1976.[10]

8. SRI LANKA

State level concern for the older persons in Sri Lanka dated back to 1944 when a Social Service Commission under the Chairmanship of Sir Ivor Jennings was appointed to look into their problems. It was probably the first country in the region to formulate a national policy for the elderly.

The Public Service Pension Scheme and the Employees Provident Fund provide social security for employees in the organized sector. Two other contributory schemes instituted by the Ministry of Social Welfare and by some banks expand the coverage base in this regard. The Ministry of Social Welfare introduced, in 1996, a Social Security and Pension Scheme for persons employed in the informal sector.

There are at present the following schemes for providing income security to the elderly:

Public Service Pension Scheme (PSPS)

The public servants who work on a permanent contract with the government are covered by the Scheme. They are generally entitled to a lump sum payment equivalent to an amount of 90 per cent of two years pension entitlement if they have worked for more than 30 years and 80 per cent if they have worked between 20-30 years. In addition they are entitled to a cash payment based on the period of service and the pay drawn. This payment is made for life.

Public Servants Provident fund Scheme (PSPF)

The officers of public service who are not entitled to pension under the PSPS can become a member of the Public Service Provident Fund.

Local Government Officers Pension Scheme (LGOPS)

This scheme is designed for the benefit of the officers of Local

Governments. It comprises of three sub-schemes:

(i) Local Government Service Pension Scheme;

(ii) Local Government Service Widows and Orphans Pension Scheme; and

(iii) Local Government Service Widowers and Orphan Pension Scheme.

Employees Provident Fund

This is the most extensive social security scheme in the country. Around 1.8 million persons working in the private sector and semi-government sector are covered under the Scheme. Under this scheme the employers and the employees contribute to the fund an amount equal to 12 per cent and 8 per cent respectively of the monthly total earnings of an employee. When the employee retires from service after attaining a prescribed age he /she can withdraw the balance in the provident fund. The balance in the PF may also be withdrawn on the death or incapacitation of the employee.

Employees Trust Fund

Under this scheme the employers contribute an amount equal to 3% of the total earnings of an employee monthly. All the members of the EPF are eligible to be members of this Fund. The Scheme provides for an oldage benefit, invalidity benefit, sickness benefit and an unemployment benefit. The original objective of the fund was to promote employer ownership of equities. But this objective is no longer being served. There is therefore a duplication between the EPF and the ETF.[11]

Approved Private Provident Funds

Under the EPF Act the Commissioner of Labour has the power to approve private provident funds for specific firms to cover its own employees. Employers and employees both contribute to the schemes. Rates vary from firm to firm but they cannot be lower than the rates at which contributions have to be made to the EPF. At the end of 1998 there were 204 APPFs with 164, 000 members.[12]

Farmers Pension Scheme/Fishermen's Pension Scheme

These schemes are also contributory, designed for the benefit of farmers and fishermen. The members become eligible for an oldage pension by qualifying after contributing for a stipulated period.

The Farmers Pension and Social Security Scheme was introduced under the Farmers Pension and social Security Benefits Scheme Act 1987. This a voluntary and contributory scheme and is funded by contributions from the members and supplemented by Government grants. Contributions are usually paid twice a year until the completion of 59 years. Membership of the Scheme is open only to subsistence farmers and agricultural labourers who are between the ages of 18 and 59. The qualifying members are entitled to the following benefits:

- A monthly pension upon reaching the age of 60 years In case of death of a pensioner the spouse will receive the pension until what would have been the pensioner's 80th year.
- In the event of permanent total disability before reaching 60 years of age, compensation not exceeding Rs.50,000 and refund of accumulated contributions together with interest or alternatively a monthly allowance from the date of permanent disablement.

The Scheme is administered by Agricultural Insurance Board established under the Agricultural Insurance Act, 1973.

Fishermen's Pension and Social Security Benefit Scheme

This scheme was established under the Fishermen's Pension and Social Security Benefit Scheme Act 1990. This Scheme is also administered by the Agricultural Insurance Board. This a voluntary Scheme funded by contributions by members supplemented by Government Grants. Membership of the Scheme is open to those living by fishing or fish farming whether at sea or in lagoons or inland water bodies provided they are in the age group of 18 to 59. Contributions are made quarterly until the completion of 59 years of age. Lump sum annual may also be made.

Pension and Social Security Benefit Scheme for Self-Employed Persons

This scheme was introduced under the Social Security Board Act 1996. It is a voluntary and contributory scheme. Any self-employed person in the age group of 18-59 in one of the approved occupations is entitled to join the scheme. The Scheme is in three parts. Under

Schedule A a member joining the scheme at age 18 has to make quarterly payments of Rs. 50 each and on retirement receives a monthly pension of Rs. 2500. Under Schedule C the member has to pay Rs. 100 a month and on retirement he will receive a monthly pension of Rs. 5000. Under Schedule D the member has to contribute Rs. 155 per month and his monthly pension on retirement will be Rs. 8000.

The main benefits under the Scheme are as follows:

- A monthly pension upon reaching 60 years of age up to the end of the month in which the contributor dies.
- In the event of permanent total disablement before reaching 60 years of age a lump sum gratuity up to Rs. 50,000 upon leaving the scheme or a periodical allowance from the date of disablement.
- In the event of permanent partial disablement before reaching 60 years of age, a lump sum gratuity up to Rs. 25,000 upon leaving the scheme or a periodical allowance from the date of disablement.
- In the event of death a gratuity up to Rs. 25,000.
- In the case of death of a contributor after receiving a pension but before reaching 80 years of age the spouse will receive the pension until what would have been the 80th year of the pensioner if the spouse is not a contributor to any scheme or not receiving or entitled to any pension. If the spouse is a contributor to any scheme or is receiving or entitled to any pension the spouse will receive the balance of the net contribution made by the contributor together with interest.

Residential Care by Government

Residential care has been provided for older persons since 1951 by the government. Currently, there are three state-run oldage homes. These accommodate olders, both men and women, who are over 60 years of age and destitute. Admissions to them are made on the recommendations of the Grama Niladhari (Village Officer) and the social service officer and on the approval of the provincial director of social services. The management of each home is by a superintendent assisted by staff. The supervision of these homes is by the respective provincial ministries through provincial social services.

Although the expenditure on maintenance to the homes is borne by the State the public too makes contributions, mainly of food, clothing, bedding and medicines in the form of alms. The other facilities available to the residents are healthcare, reading material and facilities for religious observance and pilgrimages. In the year 2000 the total expenditure allotted for the three homes amounted to Rs. 13.1 million. These homes provide care for persons over 60 years of age and destitute who do not suffer from an infectious disease at the time of admission.

Residential Care by Voluntary Organizations

The first non-government organization to establish a home for elders was the Mallika Nivasa Samithiya. This organization was formed in 1920 and it established a home for female elders the following year. Later, larger religious organisations such as the All Ceylon Buddhist Congress, the Catholic Church and the Young Men's Buddhist Association embarked on the activity.

There were a total of 89 oldage homes run by non-governmental organizations in various parts of the country at the end of the year 2000. This number comprised 11 homes for males, 12 for females and 66 for both sexes. The total number of residents in these homes was 3687.

These homes are run largely with the help of contributions made by the membership and members of the public. Contributions by the public are mostly made in kind in the form of cooked food and clothes. The homes that have been registered under the Voluntary Social Service Organisation (Registration and Supervision) Act No. 31 of 1980 are qualified to receive from the state a monthly allowance of 300 rupees per inmate. Since devolution of powers, these disbursements are made by the respective provincial councils.

In addition to the monthly allowance the homes qualify for a grant not exceeding 75,000 rupees per institution per year for improvement of building and a further 40,000 rupees for purchase of equipment and clothing. These homes are supervised by the provincial director of social services and by the social service officers under them, in order to ensure that they are maintained according to the rules and regulations of the government.[13]

References

1. Country Paper Bangladesh Presented by Mr. Md Dalil Uddin Mondal, Joiunt Secretary Ministry of Labour and Employment, Government of

People's Republic of Bangladesh, at the Seminar on Social Security for the Elderly, New Delhi September, 2000.

2. Social Security for the unorganized sector in South Asia by S.Irudaya Rajan; *International Social Security Review*, Vol.55 No.4, Oct-Dec. 2002.
3. Ibid.
4. Recent Developments in China's Social Security Reforms by Yukun Zhu, *International Social Security Review*, Vol 55 No. 4.
5. Ibid.
6. Social Security for the Elderly in China by Zhang Guo Qing, Ministry of Labour and Social Security, China.
7. National Pension Scheme in Korea: Ministry of health and Welfare, National Pension Corporation (2001).
8. " Issues in Incomes Provision for the Elderly in Malayasia" by Kevin Caraher Department of Sociology and Social Policy, University of Durham, United Kingdom: International Social Security Association Research Programme, The Year 2000 International Research Conference on Social Security: Helsinki: September 2000.
9. Social Security for the elderly by Dal Bahadur K.C., Ministry of Labour and Transport , Nepal, Paper presented at the Seminar on Social Security for the Elderly held in New Delhi in September 2000.
10. Country paper read by Mr. Farhat Hussain, Federal Secretary, Ministry of Labour Manpower and Overseas Pakistanis, at the Conference on Pension Reforms in South Asia held in November 2000 in New Delhi.
11. Reforming formal social security systems in India and Sri Lanka by Wasana Karunarathne and Randev Goswami, *International Social Security Review*, Vol 55 No.4.
12. Country paper presented by Mr. Boralugoda Sirisena at the Seminar on Social Security for the Elderly, held in September 2000 in New Delhi.
13. Social Security for the Unorganised Sector in south Asia by S.Irudaya Rajan, *International Social Security Review*, Vol.55.- 4/2002.

7

Social Security for the Elderly in India

R.K.A.SUBRAHMANYA

Social security is a basic human right. It is based on the principle that society has an obligation to provide livelihood to every one of its members by providing work to those who can work and by other means to those who cannot work. Right to work and right to social security are complementary social rights. The object of social security is thus to provide livelihood to those who cannot work and earn their living.

According to the Supreme Court, Right to Livelihood inheres the Right to Life a fundamental right enshrined in Article 21 of the Constitution of India.

The term livelihood is a broad expression comprehending all the necessities of life which enables a person "to live with human dignity", "including all those aspects of life which go to make a man's life meaningful, complete and worth living" which would be "something more than survival or animal existence."

Social Security Needs

The social security needs of the elderly consist of food, clothing, shelter, health security and above all psychological or emotional support. All these needs can be met to a large extent if the people have adequate income. Income security is therefore given preeminent position in any system of social security for the elderly. This security may be provided in cash or in kind or both.

The need for social security may be chronic or temporary. It is chronic in the case of the persons who are unemployed and who are unemployable because of their age or other disabilities. It may be temporary in the case of others. In the latter case the need for social security arises when a contingency arises such as sickness, accident, maternity, loss of employment due to retrenchment or closure of a unit, oldage or death of a breadwinner. These occurrences may be normal incidences of life or may be the result of natural or manmade disasters or catastrophes.

Universal Versus Means Tested Systems of Social security

Social security for the elderly may be universal or means tested. In a country like India universal coverage may not be practical. A targeted approach is unavoidable. People in the middle and upper middle class may not need social security. It is therefore desirable that social security programmes should concentrate on no income or low income groups of people.

The current thinking appears to be that every individual or group of individuals should make their own arrangements for meeting the various contingencies or risks of life. It should certainly be the primary objective of public policy to enable the individuals to make such arrangements. Every society would, however, have many sections of people who cannot make such arrangements, known as the excluded categories—those who are excluded from enjoying the benefits of development and are dependent on society or the State for their protection. The Constitution requires that the State should make effective provision for securing the right to public assistance in such cases including the old the disabled and the incurably sick.

Strategies for Providing Social Security

There are various ways of providing social security of which the preferred ones are social assistance and social insurance. Actually different combinations of social assistance and social insurance schemes are in vogue in different countries.

Broadly speaking social insurance types of schemes will be appropriate in respect of those for whom contributions may be made by the beneficiaries themselves or others. In respect of those for whom no contributions can be recovered social security protection will have to be provided under social assistance schemes.

Multi-tiered System of Social Security

The appropriate strategy for providing social security in India, particularly for the elderly, therefore requires classification of the people according to their economic status.

From the point of view of social security first priority has to be given to people of the last category, namely the old, the infirm and the young persons who are destitute and constitute the liability of the State and the first charge on the resources of the State. Admittedly social security for this class of people has necessarily to be provided by means of social assistance.

Above this class are those for whom social security may be provided by means partly of social insurance and partly of social assistance. Next in the order would be those for whom social security may be provided entirely on a contributory basis. Above them would be those who do not need social security being able to make their own provision for meeting the contingencies that arise including oldage.

Thus the system of social security in India would consist of a multitiered structure. Indeed, there is already such a structure though in a rudimentary form. In the first tier there is the National Social Assistance Programme and other social assistance programmes. At the second tier there are the social insurance schemes, namely, the ESI Scheme, the Schemes framed under the EPF Act, the employers' liability schemes and such others. At the next level are the numerous voluntary health insurance and oldage pension schemes which are being run by LIC, GIC, the UTI and other financial institutions. Lately a new set of schemes have appeared on the scene and they are the welfare funds, subsidised insurance schemes, self help groups, micro-credit, micro-finance and micro-insurance schemes etc meant to provide social security to the workers in the unorganised sector. Each of these tiers needs to be expanded to cover the whole population, especially the vulnerable sections.

National Social Assistance Programme

The National Social Assistance Programme consists of three separate schemes, namely, the National Oldage Pension Scheme, the National Maternity Benefit Scheme and the National Family Benefit Scheme. We are here concerned with the National Oldage Pension Scheme.

National Old-age Pension Scheme

The National Oldage Pension Scheme provides for a pension of Rs.75 per month to the old people living in conditions of destitution. This rate was fixed in 1995 and has not been revised since then despite the fact that the real value of the pension has been reduced by steadily rising prices. Some state governments have, however, on their own raised the level of old pension. Considering that the floor level of minimum wage suggested to the state governments for adoption by the Central Government is Rs. 45 per day catering to three consumption units, the amount required for bare subsistence would be Rs.15 per day per person. By this reckoning the minimum amount required for subsistence would be Rs. 450 per month per person. Granting that the amount of pension is usually limited to 50 per cent of the last wage drawn the amount of minimum pension cannot be less than Rs. 225 per month. The rate of pension payable under the National Oldage Pension is therefore totally inadequate for the subsistence of the pensioners and needs to be raised.

There are broadly three criteria for eligibility to oldage pension:

(a) Before the introduction of the NSAP the age limit varied from 60 to 65. It has now been made uniform at 65. A suggestion has been made to reduce it to 60.

(b) Before the introduction of the NSAP, in all States except Kerala and Gujarat only the destitute old were eligible for.the pension. 'Destitutes' were defined as those without any source of income and no relatives to support them. In Gujarat, however, it was provided that eligible persons should not have an income exceeding Rs. 300 per month individually or be a member of a family with an adult son the total income of which exceeds Rs. 1200. In Kerala, the relatives who support the applicant did not have a monthly income of more than Rs. 50. NSAP has allowed the States/ UTs to continue to follow the same income criteria for eligibility for oldage pension under the programme but the Central Government has reserved the right to review and to revise the criteria. No such review appears to have been done.

The income criteria for eligibility for the pensions calls for review and revision.

While destitution is the criterion for oldage pension, poverty is the criterion for other benefits under the NSAP. The Working Group on Social Security of the Economic Administration Reforms Commission had recommended that persons earning less than Rs. 2500 per annum (50 percent of the poverty line at 1979-80 prices) should be entitled to oldage pension. It is desirable that a similar criterion related to the poverty line should be adopted for the National Oldage Pension Scheme. Assuming that the estimated income at the poverty line is Rs.16,000 per annum, the income ceiling for eligibility for oldage pension may be fixed at Rs. 8000 per annum.

Annapurna

Under another scheme called Annapurna, 10 kgs of food grains per person per month free of cost will be provided to indigent senior citizens. Initially this benefit was admissible only to those persons who were eligible for oldage pension but were not presently receiving the pension and whose close children were not residing in the same village. Government has since decided that from November 2000 foodgrains will be allocated under the Annapurna Scheme to indigent old persons inclusive of those receiving old age pension from the State Governments.

The supply of foodgrains under this scheme can be regarded as supplementing the oldage pension.

Supply of Cloth

The Government of Tamilnadu has a scheme under which sarees and *dhoties* are supplied to indigent old people free of cost twice a year during Pongal and Deepavali.

It has been suggested that a similar scheme be introduced at the national level.

Integration of Schemes

It is further suggested that all such schemes may be suitably integrated so as to be complementary to each other and to meet all the basic needs of the people below the poverty line in cash or in kind. There are complaints about the implementation of the various social assistance schemes. They need to be addressed.

The ILO in its report on Social Protection for the Unorganised Sector has drawn attention to the following issues concerning implementation of social assistance schemes:

(i) to determine the criteria for eligibility (income, assets, *niradhar* status etc.),

(ii) to improve targeting and delivery by:

- (a) to assess the best modes of payment,
- (b) to design a rigorous poverty assessment method that will be the base for fixing budget ceilings at the block level,
- (c) to define a mechanism by which benefits can be adjusted for inflation, and

(iii) to link up social assistance programmes with other antipoverty programmes.

Action will have to be taken on all these lines.

Subsidised Insurance Schemes

One of the models for providing a measure of social security for workers in the unorganised sector is insurance. The Government of India as well as several state governments have launched a variety of subsidised insurance schemes for the benefit of the weaker sections of the people through the Life Insurance Corporation of India and the General Insurance Corporation of India. One of such schemes introduced through the LIC is Jeevan Suraksha a pension scheme. Another such scheme introduced through the GIC is Jeevan Arogya.

Recently, many of these schemes were discontinued and replaced by a new scheme called Janashree Bima Yojana. The new Scheme was introduced in August 2000. Under this scheme insurance benefit has been raised to Rs. 20000 for natural death, Rs. 25,000 for partial disability and Rs.50,000 for accidental death or permanent disability. The premium is Rs. 200 which is subsidised to the extent of 50 per cent; the insured person has to pay a premium of Rs. 100 per annum and the balance is paid out of the Social Security Fund maintained by the LIC.

The Government of India have also introduced another insurance scheme for the benefit of agricultural workers called Khetihar Mazdoor Bima Yojana. The introduction of this scheme was announced on 18th of May 2001 at the end of the inaugural session of the 37th Indian Labour Conference, and it is reported to have been actually launched with effect from July 1, 2001. The following benefits will be provided under the scheme:

i. Lump sum payment of Rs. 20,000 on natural death.
ii. Lump sum payment of Rs. 50,000 in case of death due to accident.
iii. Lump sum payment of Rs. 50,000 in case of permanent disability or Rs. 25,000 in case of partial disability due to accident.
iv. If the agricultural worker survives the age of 60 he will be entitled to a pension ranging from Rs. 100 to Rs. 1900 per month depending on age entry.
v. In case of death after the age of 60.

vi. On death after commencement of pension the family will be paid a lump sum amount ranging from Rs. 13,000 to Rs. 2,50,000 depending on the age of entry to the scheme.

vii. The insured person has to pay a premium of Rs. 1 per day or Rs. 365 per annum and the Central Government will pay double this amount, that is Rs 730 per annum.

The differential rates of subsidy payable under the two schemes may be open to the criticism of discrimination unless the distinction sought to be made between the different target groups can stand the test of reasonable classification. It is therefore desirable to rationalise the subsidised insurance scheme providing for a uniform rate of subsidy and for differential rates of contribution by the insured persons The scheme will be administered by project societies to be set up.

It is also desirable to extend the application of the scheme to all classes of workers in the unorganised sector over a course of time if not immediately.

It has been the experience of Insurance companies in India that however low the rates of premium may be the take up of subsidised voluntary insurance policies has not been encouraging. There is no reason to believe that the response to the new insurance schemes introduced by the LIC will be better. It would therefore be necessary to make them mandatory by linking with the welfare funds or welfare boards so that the insured persons' share of the premium is paid by the welfare fund as in the case of the groups insurance scheme for beedi workers.

Pension Insurance Schemes

In so far as workers in the organised sector are concerned retirement benefits are at present being provided through provident fund schemes. There are numerous provident fund schemes in India of which the Employees Provident Fund Scheme established under the Employees Provident Funds and Misc Provisions Act, 1952 is the largest in terms of the number of persons covered and the volume of the funds. The scheme provides for payment of contribution to the Provident Fund by the workers and their employers at a minimum of 10 per cent each. Some of the specified industries are required to pay contribution at a higher rate of 12 per cent. Till recently, the accumulation in the Provident Fund released on retirement was expected to provide income security in oldage. As however the average balance available in the individual Provident Fund accounts of the members at the time of retirement was found to be so small because of the provision permitting premature withdrawals from the fund for various purposes to be adequate to provide any such security. There was therefore a demand for introduction of a pension scheme. Eventually, the EPF scheme was restructured and an Employees Pension scheme was established. The contribution of the employers to the extent of 8.33 per cent of wages are transferred to a pension fund established under the Employees Pension Scheme. This scheme has been in force for over six years and a large number of members of the PF are now drawing pension under the Scheme. The scheme is however not popular.

The EPS has also been criticised as not viable and that it is under-funded. The current decline in interest rates is making the scheme less and less viable. There are many suggestions for reform of the Employees Pension Scheme. It seems necessary to have the scheme reviewed by an independent valuer and to put it on a sound footing.

Dave Committee Report

The Ministry of Social Justice set up a committee under the Chairmanship of SA Dave to suggest measures for providing income security in oldage to workers in the unorganised sector. The Committee has recommended the introduction of a new pension system based on individual contributions. The Government endorsed these recommendations and asked the Insurance Regulatory and Development Authority to draw up a Pension Scheme on that basis.

The main thrust of the Dave committee report is that the State as well as the employers should be relieved of the responsibility for income security of the elderly and that the new pension system should be based on contributions by the insured persons themselves. What the committee has recommended is a voluntary private pension insurance scheme. There can be no objection to the introduction of a private insurance scheme which people have the option to join or not. But it will not be a social security scheme and it cannot be a substitute for a social security scheme.

The history of social security tells us that before the introduction of social security there were private insurance schemes which provided a measure of protection against the contingencies which tended to deprive people of their income. It was however found that the workers struggling for survival from day to day had neither the means nor the motivation to save for the future and it became necessary for the State to intervene. The condition of labour in India has not changed much to warrant the suggestion that they may be required to make their own arrangements for the oldage security and that the State may be absolved of its responsibility to provide social security. Basic social security has to be provided by the State. Voluntary pension schemes can only be supplementary to the basic schemes.

Another major thrust of the Dave Committee report is that the management of pension funds should be entrusted to professional fund managers. A similar recommendations is understood to have been made by a team of experts who conducted a study of the Employees Provident Funds Scheme and the Employees Pension Scheme in India. This team has mooted the idea that the management of EPF funds should be outsourced "to private accredited fund managers under liberalised investment guidelines and appropriate regulatory oversight".

The principal argument in favour of private management of pension schemes is that private managers can obtain better investment returns. This argument is questionable in the context of the various scams and scandals that have come to light in the working of the money markets. It has been the experience of many investors that their investments in the mutual funds have mostly lost value and there has been little or no return from those investments. There is therefore a great deal of scepticism about the idea of investment of public funds by private managers .

Where a person joins a private scheme fully conscious of the risks involved he enjoys the benefit of high return when the management is able to achieve it. At the same time he should also be prepared to suffer losses if the investments fail. But where a person makes a contribution under a mandatory scheme he does so in the firm belief that his money will be safe in the hands of the government and he will not like that the investment of his hard earned money should be exposed to unnecessary risk.

Maintenance

Maintenance is a civil right available to give economic support to the needy persons from those who are liable to protect and maintain their spouse, children, parents, etc. In law, parents are bound to maintain minor children, major children, their parents, husband his wife, and vice versa. The quantum of maintenance varies depending on the economic status of the parties.

The various personal laws such as Hindu Marriage Act, 1955, the Hindu Adoption and Maintenance Act 1955, the Indian Divorce Act 1859, the Parsi Marriage Act 1954, the Shariat Laws, etc., provide for maintenance, also known as alimony or allowance. Civil courts take long time to dispose of cases. Even if a competent civil court passes a judgement and decree, execution takes months and even years due to cumbersome legal procedures. Even before the maintenance is realised, the decree holder may die of starvation.

Realising the above, the right to maintenance has been incorporated in Chapter IX of the Criminal Procedure Code (Cr.P.C).

It is a chapter for "order for maintenance of Wives, Children and Parents". Under Section 125 of the Cr. P.C., "if any person having sufficient means neglects to maintain (a) his wife unable to maintain herself, or (b) his legitimate or illegitimate minor child, whether married or not, unable to maintain itself, or (c) his legitimate or illegitimate child (not being a married) who has attained majority, where such child is, by reason of any physical or mental abnormality or injury unable to maintain itself, or (d) his father or mother, unable to maintain himself or herself, a magistrate, of the first class, may, upon proof of such neglect or refusal, order such person to make a monthly allowance for the maintenance of his wife or such child, father or mother, at such monthly rate not exceeding five hundred rupees in the whole, as such magistrate thinks fit, and to pay the same to such person as the magistrate may from time to time direct."

Thus Rs. 500 per month is allowed as maintenance. Section 125 provides the procedure to be followed and the jurisdiction of the courts. The cases could be filed in the magistrate's court within which the petitioner resides or where the parties lastly resided together, etc. Summons case procedure has to be adopted for disposal of cases. This paves way for expeditious remedies. Section 127 is for alteration in the allowance under changed circumstances, but the monthly rate of five hundred rupees in the whole should not be exceeded.

A ceiling of Rs. 500 per month towards maintenance will not prevent vagrancy which is the object of the provision. Various women's and civil rights organisations and other activists raised their voice against this ceiling. In West Bengal the amount was raised to Rs.1500.

In Tamil Nadu after a long debate with various sections of society and women's organisations and the Tamilnadu Women's Commission, it was decided to amend Cr. P.C. and remove the ceiling and to invest the power on the magistrate to grant maintenance in his discretion taking into account the capacity of the person to pay and the need of the person seeking maintenance. The Legislative Assembly unanimously passed a bill to amend the Cr. P.C. accordingly and it was sent to the Central Government for getting President's assent. In the meantime the Government changed and the bill has been withdrawn on the ground that the Central Government itself is contemplating a similar amendment.

The right approach appears to be to remove the ceiling on the amount to be paid for maintenance of dependants as was proposed by Tamilnadu and to leave it to the courts to decide the amount depending on the facts of the case.

Health Care

The elderly people are apt to develop health problems as they grow older. The National Policy for Older Persons recognizes that with advancing age old persons have to cope with health and associated problems some of which may be chronic, of a multiple nature, requiring constant attention and carry the risk of disability and consequent loss of autonomy. Several studies have pointed our varying percentages of morbidity among the elderly on account of visual, hearing, mental disabilities, diabetes, cancer, hypertension and coronary HD. There are however no separate health care services for old persons in India except the ESI and the CGHS which are applicable to a small number of persons who have been in service with the Central Government or in an insurable employment. In all other cases the old persons have to depend upon public medical services or private doctors and hospitals. The health insurance schemes of the GIC do not cover persons who are above the age of 70 and require greater attention.

Appropriate schemes would therefore need to be designed for the health care of the elderly similar to the Medicare and Medicaid programmes of the USA.

Providing Gainful Occupation to the Elderly

In order that the elderly people keep healthy it is necessary that they should remain gainfully active. Their service should therefore be utilised in various activities of the community such as manning child care centres, cultural clubs, vocational training centres etc for which they may be paid appropriate remuneration.

Indira Jai Prakash says that physical activity is inarguably the best method to keep functionally fit with aging. and that the benefits of continued activity are many. Citing the guidelines issued by the WHO for promoting physical activity, she has enumerated the various advantages of physical activity on the part of the aging people. The types of activities in which the aging population may be engaged have also been listed.

In 1982 the government of Singapore had set up a committee to study the problems of the aged and to make recommendations for dealing with them. This Committee observed:

> "Medical science has thrown greater light on the major ailments affecting today's generation of older people. One interesting finding is that inactivity causes both the body and the brain to age faster. There are two ways to keep an aged person active:
>
> (a) continued employment.
>
> (b) participation in hobbies, social, religious, family or community activities.
>
> Employment has the added advantage of enhancing an aged person's financial independence. He will be in a better position to meet two main concerns in oldage, , namely, financial security and increasing cost of medical and health care services."

The committee recommended *interalia* raising of the age of retirement. The committee also recommended that :

> "special training, job enhancement, and career development opportunities for the workers to be re-deployed must be provided; selected workers should be given opportunities for a second, third or even a fourth career."
>
> "all obstacles to the employment and re-employment of the aged should be removed and re-employment opportunities be provided either on full time, part time, flexitime, or some other special arrangements that will enable elderly workers to keep busy and continue to earn an income within their physical capabilities."

These recommendations are as valid for India as for Singapore and need to be considered for adoption suitably.

Medicare Programme

There is a Medicare National Health Insurance System in the US to provide medical care to the elderly persons. It is a federal government programme which was introduced in 1965. Under the scheme assistance is given to older and disabled people to pay for their medical costs. The scheme is in two parts. Part A is called hospitalisation insurance. It covers most of the costs of a stay in hospital as well as some follow up costs. Part B called Medical Insurance pays for the cost of doctors and outpatient care. The service is provided by certain private companies called carriers or intermediaries under contract with the government. Most of the people of the age 65 and above are covered under the scheme free of cost based on their work records. Those who are not eligible for such coverage will be covered on payment of a prescribed premium.

The medicare programme does not, however, meet the entire cost of medical care of the elderly. It does not pay for certain types of costs and services. It is said that broadly speaking it covers only 50 per cent of the medical costs. The balance has to be paid for by the insured persons themselves by way of yearly deductibles or co-payments. There is therefore another scheme called Medicaid under which those who cannot make such payments are given assistance. This is a state level programme which varies from state to state. In many States, Medicaid covers costs which are not paid for by Medicare. including the premium for Medicare, the annual deductibles etc. A similar programme needs to be introduced in India.

Long Term Care

With the growth of the population of the aged, the associated problem of caring for the aged is becoming increasingly important. Lately, long term care of the elderly in some of the developed countries has been systematized in the form of social care insurance as a part of social security. It has been reported that in 1991, in Germany, approximately one-third of the social security expenditures was devoted to care provision. The concept of care dependency is distinct from treatment for illness and covers help with daily tasks that do not fall under any medical treatment plan, e.g., personal hygiene, feeding, mobility or housework.

In the US, there are many home health-care agencies providing care for patients who donot need high level hospital care but still require part time nursing or physical therapy.

There may be terminally ill patients who cannot be cured of their maladies but need comfort so that they may die in peace. Hospices provide such care.

There are many voluntary organisations providing medical care as well as long term care and hospice care to the elderly in India but they are not adequate. Considering the size of the elderly population in India their care cannot be left entirely to voluntary organisations. The state has to come in big way and support private efforts so that they may expand their services.

Oldage Homes

While ordinarily the elderly persons live with their children and grand children, circumstances are developing in such a way that many of them have had to live independently or under institutional care. Sometimes the health condition of the persons may be such that the concerned families may not be able to provide the necessary care. In some cases there may be no family at all. At the worst, the families might have abandoned them. The elderly persons would need institutional care in such circumstances. A WHO seminar of Health experts is reported to have concluded as follows:

> "The emergent need for some basic provision of institutional care is now evident in most countries of the region (Western Pacific countries). The seminar identified the need for Governments to take account of this trend to enact legislation and regulations to ensure good quality, appropriate, equitable, and cost-efficient provision of institutional services whether by the Government, non-Governmental organizations or the private sector".

The National Policy for Older Persons recognizes this need. The national policy is to consider institutional care as the last resort when personal circumstances are such that old age homes become absolutely necessary. The policy provides for giving assistance to voluntary organizations for construction and maintenance of oldage homes.

According to information available there are over 300 oldage homes in this country. Some of these are maintained by the State Governments and most are run by non-Government organizations with assistance from Government. There are also some institutions run by private charitable institutions without any assistance from

Government. The total number of inmates in these institutions is about 15,000. Assuming that at least 1 percent of the aged require institutional care, facilities would have to be created for providing institutional care to about fifteen lakh persons. It has been reported that nearly 5 per cent of the elderly live in institutions abroad. It is doubtful if voluntary organizations will come forward to set up so many oldage homes. There is therefore no alternative to the Central and State Governments taking the initiative to set up their own homes in sufficient numbers.

One cannot be content with the setting up of the homes. The quality of service provided in these homes needs to be monitored. The existing arrangements in this regard are less than adequate. It is therefore necessary to establish a well organised regulatory system to ensure that standards are maintained and exploitation avoided.

Emotional Support to the Elderly: Strengthening the Family System

Institutional care cannot be a total substitute for family care. The Committee on the Problems of the Aged referred to above made certain significant observations in this regard. The committee observed:

> "Aging is not only a physical process but also a state of mind. The physical process can be slowed down by advances in medical science and by keeping good health. The state of mind also affects the rate at which a person ages. A person is to a great extent, conditioned by how old he feels he is, rather than how old he actually is. Such feelings are usually fostered by attitudes of society. Today, large sections of society still deem the elderly to be group of persons who should be classified with the sick and the disabled, who are no longer fit for employment or capable of being retrained or re-educated to fit into new jobs. Such myths are often encouraged by media coverage of the elderly as weak and dependant. For, from being a burden, the elderly should be recognised as possessing experience, skills, knowledge, talent and wisdom, all of which are invaluable national assets. They should therefore not be isolated from the mainstream of society."

> "Home for the aged can be built but experience all over the world has shown that this is not the kind of place where the elderly should be kept. The elderly need to remain active, to know that they still have a part to play in the family or community to which

they can make a useful contribution. They still need to feel wanted and loved. To put them in institutions is to let them know that they are being discarded. The support and care must come from the heart, with feelings of sympathy affection and compassion."

The committee had therefore recommended that concerted effort must therefore be made to preserve and strengthen the traditional family system. "Instead of admitting the elderly to institutions in the false hope that the problem will stop there, the government should adopt a national policy aimed at keeping every elderly individual physically and mentally fit and active so that he can retain his normal living arrangements as long as possible."

There can therefore no better way to provide the emotional support the elderly need as they grow older.

8

Current Issues in Pension Reform

MUKUL G. ASHER

The main objective of any social security system is the provision on a sustainable basis of a socially adequate and equitable retirement protection system while simultaneously minimizing adverse effects on economic efficiency, fiscal consolidation and flexibility, incentives to work and save and international competitiveness. In designing, implementing, and reforming a social security system, it is therefore essential to recognize the inescapable need for trade-offs among the above factors. In particular, two extremes should be avoided, one, focusing only on the needs (or wants) of the elderly and the other, only on minimizing budgetary costs of providing retirement security.

There are six core functions which any provident or pension fund organization needs to perform (Ross, 2000). These are the reliable collection of contributions, taxes and other receipts; the payment of benefits in a correct way; the timely repayment in case of pre-retirement loans; the effective financial management and productive investment of the assets; the maintenance of an effective communication network, which also includes development of accurate data and records-keeping mechanisms; and the provision of adequate support for all these activities, including the production of financial statements and reports. The management information reports are tied to providing effective and reliable governance, fiduciary responsibility, transparency, and accountability.

The provident and pension fund organizations need to approach their tasks in a professional manner and benchmark themselves against best practices prevailing both nationally and internationally. The gap between best performing and worst performing organizations in a given country is often disturbingly wide. Narrowing this gap should therefore have a high priority. It is important to note that while the investment function is important, it should not be overemphasized nor made overly

---

Professor of Economics and Public Policy, Public Policy Programme, National University of Singapore.

complex, particularly when there is significant scope for improvement in other core functions. This however does not imply that only debt investment portfolio is optimal and that a provident or pension fund organization can dispense with the task of developing in-house investment management expertise.

Policymakers and society as a whole have a strong interest in ensuring not only that each provident and pension fund organization is managed professionally and competently, but also that their broader concerns about economic effects and future development of the social security system of the country are also addressed. This requires them to take a system-wide perspective to minimize any adverse economic impact of the operations of the provident fund and pension scheme on fiscal (and macro-economic) sustainability, on labour markets, and on international competitiveness. In addition, they have a stake in enhancing literacy in pension economics and issues concerning the stakeholders, including trustees of provident fund and pension fund schemes, the policymakers themselves, the fund members, and the service providers. The educational function and nurturing of the various components of provident and pension fund industry deserve considerable emphasis in the developing countries.

The main objective here is to highlight key pension reform issues facing the organizations and policymakers dealing with social security systems in the Asian and Pacific countries. The focus of the discussion is primarily on low and middle-income countries in this region. Many, though not all, of these countries have a large informal sector requiring separate arrangements as conventional provident fund and pension schemes are not well suited to those without employers. In addition, many of these countries have a dualistic social security system. Under such a system, a small group is able to obtain a higher level and wider extent of retirement protection than the rest of the population, often without any or only a token contribution. Typically, civil servants, workers of state enterprises, and members of armed forces have enjoyed such superior protection[1].

The next section provides an overview of the selected demographic indicators of the world and Asia. The overview is designed to highlight the point that the focus of social security challenge is increasingly shifting to Asia. How Asia responds to this challenge will have considerable ramifications on the extent to which the pension challenge is met by the world. This is followed by a discussion of the main issues in pension reforms facing the Asian and

Pacific countries. There are four issues discussed in this section. The first issue involves a need in varying degrees to enhance professionalism in provident and pension fund organizations and to ensure that a system-wide perspective is undertaken. In the Asian and Pacific countries, social security reforms are only just beginning to emerge as an important public policy issue. The second issue is the reform of civil service pensions. The third issue concerns reforming provident fund and pension scheme arrangements for private sector workers. The fourth issue concerns enhancing social protection for those in the informal sector. The final section provides the concluding observations.

Demographic Indicators of the World and Asia

It may be useful to briefly recapitulate the evidence on demographic trends in the world and Asia (Table 8.1).

- In the year 2000, about 0.6 billion people, 10 per cent of the world's population, were over 60 years of age.
- By 2025, this number will nearly double to 1.18 billion, around 15 percent of the world's population; and by 2050, the number will be 1.96 billion, around 21.1 percent of the world's population.
- In 2000, the elderly (i.e., those above 60 years of age) female population was 11.1 percent of the world population while the corresponding male population was 8.9 percent. By 2025, 16.3 percent of the female population and 13.6 per cent of the male population will be elderly. By 2050, the number will nearly double to reach 22.7 percent of the female population and 19.4 percent of the male population of the world.
- In 2000, the life expectancy at 60 years of age for the total population was 18.8 years. The number was 20.4 years for the female population and 17.0 years for the male population. By 2025, these numbers will be 21.0 years for the total population: 22.8 years for the female population and 19.1 per cent for the male population. As a result, gender issues are intricately linked to old-age social security arrangements.
- Most of the growth will take place in developing countries, over half of it in Asia and more than a quarter in China alone.
- Many developing countries will have an 'old' demographic

profile at a much lower level of per capita income than the industrial countries. Thus, by the middle of this century, the elderly in China will number around 250 million and in India, around 180 million. These are staggeringly large numbers.

- The problem in the developing countries will not just be related to the level of the elderly population but also to the rapid pace of ageing as well. For example, while in the United States it took 81 years for the population aged 60 years and over to rise from 10 to 20 per cent of the national population, the corresponding increase will take only 18 years in Singapore, 23 years in Korea, 24 years in Thailand, 26 years in Indonesia and 27 years in China and Taiwan.
- Almost half of the world's population is now in countries with fertility levels below replacement rate (less than 2.1 children per woman). These include nearly all countries in Western Europe, Russia, many parts of eastern and central Europe, major parts of Asia including China, several states in India, Canada, Australia, and parts of Latin America. The United States is a significant exception largely due to its willingness and ability to absorb net immigration over a substantial period.
- Thus, most of the high-income countries, and several low and middle-income countries have fertility levels below replacement rate.
- The above implies that over time the absolute population will begin to fall, if net immigration is not taken into account. These trends, if they materialize, will have profound economic and political consequences for the countries concerned. Singapore is already grappling with this issue as its total fertility rate. TFR, defined as the number of children a woman in child-bearing period is expected to produce, has been below the replacement rate since 1975: about a quarter of its workforce is foreign and the net immigration is high bringing about subtle but profound changes in society (Asher, 2002). Japan is experiencing even more serious symptoms, with its population expected to begin declining in the next decade (Takayama, 2002, Fig. 1 p12).
- Life expectancy has also been rising. It is estimated that life expectancy at birth for men in the world as a whole will rise from 61 years in 1998 to 67 years in 2025, and for women

from 65 years to 72 years. In high-income countries, the average age of women may soon be above 80 years of age. Gender issues are inevitably tied up with social security. Individual ageing will also significantly impact on health costs.

- The consequences on financing the elderly will also be profound. In countries such as China, the enterprise-based social security system acts as a severe constraint in state-enterprise reform essential for a transition to a more market-consistent economy (Asher and Newman, 2002).

Table 8.1. Selected Demographic Indicators: World and Asia

Indicator	2000		2025		2050	
	World	Asia	World	Asia	World	Asia
Total population (millions)	6056.7 (100)	3772.3 (62.3)	7936.7 (100)	4776.6 (60.2)	9322.3 (100)	5428.2 (58.2)
Population above 60 years (millions)						
Total	605.8 (100)	322.2 (53.2)	1186.9 (100)	703.4 (59.3)	1963.8 (100)	1226.7 (62.5)
Male	271.4 (100)	151.4 (55.8)	543.4 (100)	330.2 (60.8)	902.2 (100)	569.6 (63.1)
Female	334.3 (100)	170.6 (51)	643.6 (100)	373.2 (58)	1061.6 (100)	656.8 (61.9)
Median age (years)	26.5	26.2	32.0	33.1	36.2	38.3
Dependency ratio (%)	10.9	9.2	15.9	14.9	24.7	26.1
Sex Ratio (men/100 women)						
60 +	81.2	88.8	84.4	88.5	85.0	86.8
80 +	53.1	61.2	57.7	60.9	60.7	62.2
Total fertility rate (TFR)[a]	2.7	2.5	2.3	2.1	2.1	2.1
Life expectancy at 60 years[b]						
Total	18.8	18.1	21.0	20.5	22.2	21.8
Male	17.0	16.6	19.1	18.7	20.2	19.9
Female	20.4	19.7	22.8	22.3	24.1	23.1
Labor force participation (+ 65) %						
Total	19.9	27.2	18.8	24.5	17.9	22.3
Male	32.9	43.5	30.2	38.4	28.1	34.2
Female	10.4	13.4	10.1	12.7	10.0	12.2

Source: http://www.un.org/esa/population/publications/worldageing19502050/index.htm

Notes: a) Number of children per woman of child bearing age.

b) Data for five-year intervals, 2000-2005, 2025-2030, and 2045-2050.

The above overview suggests that Asia is increasingly emerging as a focus of demographic challenges facing the world.

Current Issues

The discussion in this section is organized around the following four issues: achieving professionalism and a system-wide perspective; effecting civil service pension reform; reforming pensions for private sector employees; and addressing social security needs of the informal sector. The discussion is based on the premise that globalization and related technological changes have made the provision of adequate social safety nets more imperative as well as more difficult and complex (Rodrik, 1999).

Achieving Professionalism and a System-wide Perspective

In nearly all the countries in the Asian and Pacific region, each component of the social security system is operating essentially independently with wide divergence in regulatory regimes and supervisory bodies. Often, the provident fund or pension fund organization has operational as well as regulatory roles. There is also little pressure to benchmark against best practices and little transparency. The legislation governing the scheme is often outdated and while specific design provisions have been introduced on an ad hoc basis, they often adversely impact on the effectiveness of the organization. The provision that details the design and implementation can significantly alter the effects of the social security system on the individual and on the economy but this is often not well understood. Moreover, there is often no agency in charge to ensure that the provident or pension fund organization adheres to sound practices. In many countries, including the transition economies, the pension fund management of the state enterprises in some cases is not conducive to the provision of promised benefits. This is also the case with private sector occupational plans.

The above may be illustrated in the case of Sri Lanka.

As shown in Figure 1, the formal social security system of Sri Lanka has several components. Private sector workers have access to the Employees' Provident Fund (EPF), the Employees' Trust Fund (ETF), and the Approved Private Provident Funds (APPF). The government sector workers are covered by the Public Service Pension Scheme (PSPS) and the Public Service Provident Fund (PSPF). In

Figure 1: Formal socal security system of Sri Lanka

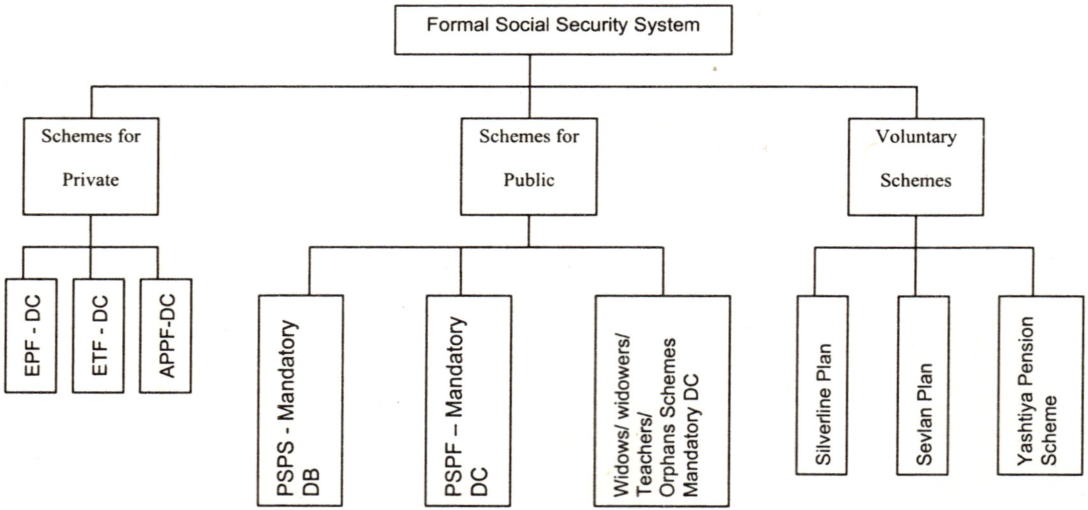

Notes: EPF: Employees Provident Fund; ETF: Employees rust Fund; Approved Privat Provident Funds (APPF); DC: defined contribution; DB: defined benefit; Public Service Pension Scheme (PSPS); Public Service Provident Fund (PSPF).
Source: Karunarathne and Goswami, 2002. p. 95.

addition, there are voluntary retirement schemes which are available to any individual with the requisite resources.

The EPF, which is currently under the Ministry of Labour, is the dominant organization for private sector workers, although some responsibilities, particularly the management of investments are undertaken by the Central Bank. The voluntary schemes are run by various banks, and therefore fall under the jurisdiction of the Central Bank which is the banking regulator. As Sri Lanka's life insurance industry becomes more developed, the pension products of these companies will fall under the insurance regulator. The public sector schemes are under the jurisdiction of the Ministry of Finance.

There is therefore little coordination among those operating the different schemes and different components of the social security system in Sri Lanka. While Figure 1 does not depict the arrangements in the informal sector, there appears to be little coordination between the social security arrangements in the formal and informal sectors.

The provident or pension fund organization operates without any formal requirement that they function with a high degree of professionalism, transparency and accountability. There is no centre of responsibility for taking a system-wide perspective and for ensuring that the economic costs of providing a given level of social security benefits are minimized. The investment portfolio of the EPF consists almost entirely of government bonds and there has been little attempt to ensure that contractual savings are translated into economically productive investments.

This lack of coordination, as illustrated by the case of Sri Lanka, is also evident in the Association of South East Asian Nations (ASEAN) countries (Asher, 2002a), and in India (Asher, 2002b). In many countries in the region, the nature of the political economy has been such that individuals who are both independent and professional have often been not given opportunities to serve as directors of provident and pension fund boards and as members of investment panels. As a result, political risk has been high. In several countries in the region, such as India and Sri Lanka, there is a close link between financing of government expenditure and provident fund flows. This not only adds to the political risk, but hampers market base allocation of savings for investments. This suggests that such a risk is not confined to only defined benefit PAYG schemes.

There is therefore a strong case for considering the setting up of an independent regulator for provident fund and pension schemes.

The proposed provident funds and pension schemes authority should ensure that each organization, including those for public sector employees, are managed professionally with a high degree of fiduciary responsibility, transparency and accountability. In many countries in the region, particularly in south Asia, the proposed authority will need to ensure that there is a gradual de-linking of the use of contractual savings for financing government deficits in an unsustainable and non-transparent manner. The need for professionalism is as strong for the public sector organizations as it is for the private sector. To the extent that certain pension products, such as those provided by insurance companies or mutual funds are already regulated by a duly constituted independent authority, the proposed provident fund and pension scheme authority would need to closely coordinate with it but it should retain responsibility for the overall economic and financial viability of the social security system and ensure the system's future development. The proposed authority should also encourage country specific empirical research on pension issues. This is essential because often policies, programmes, and measures have been advocated and sometimes implemented on the basis of extremely superficial lessons drawn from other countries at different stages of development of the economy in general and social security systems in particular.

Civil Service Pension Reform

There are two main reasons why civil service pension reform has acquired greater urgency in the Asian and Pacific countries.

First, globalization and associated volatility in financial and capital flows have made the task of attaining macro-economic sustainability, of which fiscal consolidation and flexibility are vital components, both more urgent and more complex. Civil service pension arrangements in many countries in the region were introduced when the government paid relatively low wages although it provides job security. However, over time, government wages have been increased considerably, as well as defined benefit pensions paid to civil servants improved, often without any or with only a small contribution. Moreover, those benefiting from the civil service pension arrangements (and also the civil service health benefits) have themselves often been responsible for formulating the rules without any outside authority safeguarding the public interest. This suggests that civil service provident fund and pension schemes need to be covered under an overall regulatory umbrella and must follow similar requirements as other components of the pension fund. It is therefore not surprising that in many countries in the region, civil servants enjoy superior protection. Even in health care, increased life expectancy, particularly of the civil servants as a group, will significantly impact on the costs in the future. This aspect of future fiscal liabilities has not received as much attention as it deserves.

Second, the dualism in the social security system that exists between private sector employees and those in public sector enterprises has become less acceptable on both political and economic grounds. Such dualism hampers much needed rationalization of the role of the state and the market. It also hampers labour mobility as pensions and health benefits of civil servants and state enterprise workers often act as a barrier to a shift to the private sector. Greater labour mobility between sectors could facilitate re-balancing the role of the state and the market.

The above points may be illustrated by a case study of civil service pensions in Malaysia.

The Case of Malaysia

In Malaysia, officers in the public service, employees of statutory bodies and local authorities, judges, members of parliament and the administration, political secretaries, and the armed forces are eligible to receive pensions under various legislative acts. Article 74, Ninth Schedule, List 1, paragraph 6d of the Federal List of Malaysia's Constitution stipulates that pensions be a federal matter. Protection of pension rights is enshrined in the constitution under Article 147. Section 3(1) of the Pensions Act 1980 however stipulates that the grant of a pension is only a matter of eligibility and not an absolute right. Nevertheless, the above constitutional provisions would need to be taken into account in any radical reform of civil service pensions.

A public sector employee must complete at least three years of service to be eligible for pensions. During this period, the employee is required to contribute to the Employees Provident Fund (EPF). Since 1991, government employees have had the choice of joining the EPF or the Pensions' Scheme. The pensionable civil servants are allowed to withdraw their own contributions to the EPF before reaching the age of 55 years. The contributions to the EPF of the Government as an employer for pensionable civil servants are transferred to the Pensions Trust Fund (PTF) which was established in 1991 to ensure payment of pension benefits to civil servants. The armed forces administer their own pension fund separately. But its financing is similar to that of civil servants.

The retirement age of 55 years is rather low compared to life expectancy at birth of 70.4 years for males and 75.3 years for females in 2002 (www.statistics.gov.org/english/framesetkeystats.htm). Government employees are eligible for two types of retirement benefits, namely, service pensions and service gratuity. Employees are not required to contribute for these two benefits.

Service pensions

This applies to the pensionable officer who retires according to the standard rules. Under these rules, any employee who leaves government employment before reaching retirement age forgoes all his/her accumulated pension rights. The pensions are thus not portable. This provision discourages labour mobility from the public to the private sector. The monthly pension is estimated on the basis of the following formula:

$$1/600 \times \text{total completed months of reckonable service} \times \text{last drawn salary}$$

The monthly pension is subject to a ceiling of 50 per cent of the last drawn salary. The monthly pension is not automatically indexed, but is adjusted from time to time according to the framework provided by the Pensions Adjustment Act 1980. Thus, in the year 2000 budget, pensions for the civil servants were increased by 10 percent, identical to the rise in the salary of civil servants.

Service Gratuity

This is a lump-sum payment (in addition to the monthly pension) given to the pensionable officer upon retirement. The amount is calculated as follows:

$$7.5\ \% \times \text{total completed months of reckonable service} \times \text{last drawn salary}$$

There are also provisions for derivative pensions (i.e., survivor's benefits), derivative gratuity; disability pensions; dependent's pensions (when an officer dies in the course of performing official duties); and alimentary allowances.

In addition to the above pension-related benefits, pensioners and members of their family are also eligible for extensive medical benefits, while all employees are eligible for subsidized housing loans.

Table 8.2 provides data concerning the number of persons receiving retirement benefits under the above schemes.

Based on this table, the following observations may be made:

- The number of pension recipients has been rising quite rapidly at an average annual compound growth rate (AACGR) of

Table 8.2: Malaysia's expenditure for pensions and gratuities, 1981 to 1999

Year	Total Pension recipients (Number)	Toatl expen-diture	Nominal GDP	Total expen-diture	TPR	Average amount per pensioner
1981	107490	583.9	57613	1.01	107.49	5432
1982	116431	586.6	62579	0.94	116.431	5038
1983	127206	628.5	69941	0.9	127.206	4941
1984	139025	680.2	79550	0.86	139.025	4893
1985	156018	775.5	77547	1	156.018	4971
1986	169670	833.1	71594	1.16	169.67	4910
1987	185161	939.2	79625	1.18	185.161	5072
1988	197410	960.2	90861	1.06	197.41	4864
1989	209786	1074.7	102451	1.05	209.786	5123
1990	224053	1154.2	115701	1	224.053	5151
1991	239910	1306.8	132381	0.99	239.91	5447
1992	252805	1435.6	148537	0.97	252.805	5679
1993	272806	1712.3	165206	1.04	272.806	6277
1994	294213	2046.4	190274	1.08	294.213	6956
1995	312855	2077.3	218671	0.95	312.855	6640
1996	345686	2673.8	249503	1.07	345.686	7735
1997	362667	2846.2	275367	1.03	362.667	7848
1998	386426	2884.9	279816	1.03	386.426	7466
1999	n/a	3039.1	n/a	n/a		n/a
AACGR (1981-98)	9.4	10.4	11	n/a		1.78

Note: * approvals
n/a: not available
AACGR: Average Annual Compound Growth Rate

Calculated from the formula r= ((1+rA) ^ (1/t))-1; where rA = aggregate return over t years (annual rates are aggregated by taking their product for t years).
Sources: Calculated from the data in Malaysia, Pension Division, Public Service Department, 1999, The Public Sector Pension Scheme in Malaysia.

9.4 per cent during the 1981-98 period. In 1998, the total number of pension recipients was equivalent to 44.2 per cent of government sector employees or 4.3 per cent of the total labour force. Even if only those receiving service pensions are included, the corresponding ratios were 32.1 per cent and 3.1 per cent, respectively.

- For the 1981-98 period, total expenditure on pensions and gratuities increased at an annual rate of 10.4 per cent, slightly lower than the 11.0 per cent for the nominal GDP. The ratio of pension's expenditures to the GDP ratio has remained at about 1.0 per cent of GDP during this period. However, expenditure on pensions and gratuities was 5.3 per cent of total operating expenditures of all levels of government, up from 4.5 per cent in 1993.The fiscal burden would be even higher if health benefits for the pensioners were included.
- The Malaysian government has been able to keep in remarkable check the expenditure per pensioner as shown in the last column of Table 2. This is indicated by the AACGR of only 1.78 during this period, substantially lower than for total pension recipients for total expenditure, and for GDP. In 1998, average pension at RM 7466 was only 62 percent of per capita income.

The full impact of rapid expansion in government employment during the 1970s as a result of the New Economic Policy designed to increase the share of the Bumiputra (Sons of the Soil) community in the economy on pensions expenditure is also yet to be fully felt. A study assessing the future contingent pension liabilities of the government and its incorporation in the fiscal policy may be an essential first step towards an assessment of the sustainability of the current arrangements.

Financing of civil service pensions in Malaysia

The pension benefits outlined above do not require any contribution from the employees. The pension expenditure is wholly borne by the Federal Government through an annual budgetary appropriation charged to the Federal Consolidated Fund. The statutory bodies and local authorities are required to make monthly contributions to the PTF at the rate of 17.5 per cent of the monthly salary of pensionable employees.

The PTF, while an improvement over yearly allocations from the budget practiced in other countries in the region such as Sri Lanka and India, is managed by the Accountant General's Office under the Ministry of Finance. The initial contribution of RM 0.5 billion to the PTF came from the accumulated budgetary surpluses. The rationale for the PTF is to make pension obligations of the government transparent and to separate the investment management of the pension balances from general government accounts. It also however ensures that resources to meet pension claims of civil servants have already been set aside. The assets of the PTF in mid 1998 (latest period for which data are available) were RM 11.0 billion (3.9 per cent of 1998 GDP). Unfortunately, the PTF does not publish data on its investment portfolio and returns and various characteristics of beneficiaries. It is therefore not possible to assess its investment policies and performance. This is an area where greater transparency is required.

The PTF however does not alter the defined benefit (DB) and non-contributory nature of the pension arrangements for civil servants. The pertinent question is whether such an arrangement is fiscally sustainable, particularly when the potential increases in health care benefits for the pensioners are also considered.

With some variations, the Malaysian civil service pension arrangements are typical of those found in many Asian and Pacific countries such as India, Sri Lanka, and Indonesia. Some of the countries in the region, such as India, also provide additional benefits to civil servants. These include mandatory savings in government provident fund; permitting accumulated leave at the time of retirement to be converted into monetary benefits; choice of lump sum payment of a portion of the pension, called commutation (often at overly generous discount rates); price and/ or wage indexation; and pensions to families after death of the pensioner. Unlike Malaysia, however, these countries have not experienced strong growth and a healthy fiscal situation over a sustained period.

These countries may consider examining reasons for Malaysia's success for keeping pension benefit per pension recipient at reasonable levels. Lack of automatic indexation has been a contributory factor in Malaysia's success. Therefore, the consequences of not undertaking civil service pension reform in these countries will be even more serious. Pension reforms to be affective will need to apply to both existing and new employees. In countries where extensive benefits of the type noted above are provided to civil servants, parametric reforms have the potential to have rationalized pensions, and obtain substantial savings in pension expenditure. The parametric reforms also have the advantage of not impacting on the right to pension, which has been upheld by the courts in some countries, such as India and Sri Lanka.

Reforming the Social Security System for Private Sector Employees

There are several areas not discussed earlier, which merit attention as the current social security arrangements for private sector employees are reviewed. Reform in these areas could assist in improving the current modest level of replacement rates in Southeast Asia (Asher, 2002a) and South Asia (Karunarathne and Goswami, 2002).

First, the key challenge for provident and pension fund organizations in many countries is to justify the high administrative compliance and economic costs which they impose on the rest of the society in relation to the benefits and the level and quality of services provided by them. There is therefore an urgent need for benchmarking administration and compliance costs of provident and pension fund organizations along with their service levels and quality. In some countries, e.g., Indonesia, the process of crediting the mandatory savings of provident fund members is unduly cumbersome, with a long time lag before contributions are credited (Asher, 2002a). Such benchmarking will require organizational change, but will be difficult to undertake without leadership commitment. Low levels of organizational capacity, including the absence of application of information technology, often constrains expansion of membership and active contributors to the mandatory provident and pension funds.

Second, in several countries, rationalization of design features needs to be considered. Thus, in several countries such as the Philippines, India, Sri Lanka, and Malaysia, pre-retirement withdrawals permitted for housing, health care and other purposes tend to detract significantly from the basic objective of retirement schemes. In some countries, the design of some of the pre-retirement withdrawals has proved to be counterproductive as illustrated by the scheme for withdrawal for the purchase of computers from the mandatory provident fund in Malaysia. In some countries, such as India, those earning above covered wages are nevertheless permitted to claim unlimited deduction from income tax of contributions paid to private voluntary provident funds. This has led to an unnecessary reduction of tax revenue and constraint on the growth of the mandatory national provident fund.

Third, in any accumulation scheme, investment policies and performance should enable the power of compound interest to be realized. However, provident and pension funds in many countries have been hampered by regulatory constraints and by lack of expertise in modern investment management. These have been exacerbated by the limitations of the domestic financial and capital markets, resulting in the high transaction costs of investments. While some countries such as Thailand may be at a stage where modest international diversification may be considered, many countries have not yet reached that stage. The importance of increasing the supply of investment quality obligations and equity instruments needs to be emphasized to a greater extent. The extensive role currently played by implicit and explicit guarantees of principal and of returns needs to be reviewed. The demand for issuing inflation-indexed government bonds should be resisted, particularly by the countries with real fiscal health.

Fourth, there is a need to consider options other than the lump-sum withdrawals currently prevalent in many countries. The role of life insurance companies and mutual funds could be encouraged to provide pension products, subject to appropriate supervision. India has made an encouraging start in that direction.

Social Security in the Informal/Unorganized Sector

Most of the individuals in the informal or unorganized sectors are quite vulnerable to a wide variety of economic shock (Abada, 2001, p. 3666). There are four broad avenues for enhancing social security to individuals in the informal or unorganized sector. First, for most of the individuals in this sector, budgetary programmes targeted at the elderly poor are likely to be a major source of support. It is therefore essential to focus on improving the effectiveness of the current programmes aimed at this group. The funding of the budgetary programme may be aided by channeling part of the savings from pension reforms in the formal sector to them. Fiscal consolidation and flexibility are thus essential to enhance economic security in the informal sector.

Second, it is well known that the most important macro-economic variable in economic security is the growth rate trend. Higher growth is especially important to those in the informal sector. In addition, measures designed to raise the elasticity of employment with respect to GDP, reform property rights of the poor, and lower the legal and illegal transaction costs of engaging in informal sector business could help enhance their economic security.

Third, when there are identifiable relatively large groups such as fishermen, small farmers in a particular area, workers primarily engaged in home production in a local industry, then micro-insurance, group insurance based schemes, and social funds may have merit (Abada, 2001). The design and implementation however ultimately determine the extent of success of such schemes. The Southeast Asian region has considerable recent experience in instituting social safety programmes as a result of the 1997 economic crisis. Their experience could serve as a base for designing more effective programmes (Whiteford, 2002). The approach of the Asian Development Bank to social protection in the informal sector by various Asian sub-regions has been summarized by Ortiz (2002, Table 2, p. 279). In addition to a budgetary social expenditure review, she also emphasizes the role of institutions and the political economy (2002, pp. 280-283).

The fourth avenue is to develop specific programmes to improve the level of assets and skills of individuals in this sector and assist them in applying the available stock of knowledge and technology to address their specific concerns such as asymmetric information often experienced in selling their products.

Conclusion

It is only relatively recently that social security reform has emerged as an important public policy concern in many countries in Asia and the Pacific. Globalization, the need for fiscal consolidation and flexibility, and the demographic trends have been important contributory factors in this emergence. Professional and technical expertise on pension issues is now relatively well-developed, but applying this expertise and drawing lessons which are appropriate in a specific context has not proved to be an easy task. To enhance professionalism and ensure that a system-wide perspective is adopted in social security policy, consideration should be given to constituting a provident or pension fund authority. It should regulate all components of the social security system and perform a developmental and educational role. Indeed, a political consensus to pension reforms is vital as the difficult issue of civil service pension reform needs to be urgently addressed.

Notes

1. This however is not meant to imply that in all the Asian and Pacific countries, pension provisions for civil servants enable them to maintain a regular standard of living. But if the strong rationale of a multi-tier system is accepted, then it is not desirable to provide replacement rate from just one tier.

References

Abada, J., 2001, Micro and area-based schemes: Theoretical background, in Ortiz, I. (ed.) *Social Protection in Asia and the Pacific* (Manila, Asian Development Bank), pp. 365-406.

Asher, M., 2002(a), Southeast Asia's social security systems: Need for system-wide perspective and professionalism, *International Social Security Review, 55, No.4*, pp 71-88.

—, 2002(b), Case for a provident and pension funds authority, in *Economic and Political Weekly*, 378, pp. 688-689.

Asher, M. and Newman, D., 2002, Private pensions in Asia: An assessment of eight systems, in *Regulating private pension schemes: Trends and challenges*. Private Pension Series, No. 4 (Paris, Organization for Economic Cooperation and Development), pp. 51-104.

Karunarathne, W. and Goswami, R., 2002, Reforming formal social security systems in India and Sri Lanka, *International Social Security Review, 55, No. 4*, pp 89-106.

Kuptsch, C., 2001, Social security privatization: different context-different discourse, in Scheil-Adlung, X (ed.) *Building Social Security: The challenge of privatization* (New Brunswick, Transaction Publishers), pp. 3-18.

Ortiz, I., 2002, Reforming social security protection system in Asia and the Pacific: A perspective from the ADB, in P. Whiteford (ed.), *Towards Asia's Sustainable Development: The role of social protection* (Paris, OECD), pp. 263-296.

Rodrik, Dani, 1999, Why is there so much economic insecurity in Latin America?, available from: *http://ksghome.harvard.edu/~.drodrik.academic.ksg/papers.html*

Ross, S.G., 2000, Building pension institutions: Administrative issues, in *Proceedings of the Third APEC Regional Forum on Pension Fund Reform* (Bangkok), pp. 120-132.

Whiteford, P., "Introduction" in P. Whiteford (ed.), *Towards Asia's Sustainable Development: The role of social protection* (Paris, OECD), pp. 9-20.

9

Legislated and other Benefit Plans Assessment and Suggestions

NALIN THAKOR

Considering the magnitude of the issues involved, low income level of over a third of India's population, it seems appropriate to limit the initial effort to initiating a modest health care and pension programme.

General

1. A review or a proposal for recasting or for developing a new legislated benefits program must recognize recent developments, emerging trends and experiences of other countries especially in other comparable countries.
2. More important developments and trends that need to be recognized are :
   (a) Declining role of joint family and other traditional arrangements for taking care of old and unfortunate individuals.
   (b) Increasing number of smaller nuclear families and of working spouses.
   (c) Technological and organizational changes that involve meaningful changes in skill requirements. Also, speed of such changes.
   (d) Declining period of contributory membership of benefit plans largely because of
      (i) Increase in duration of initial education and duration of working life:
      (ii) Increasing mobility because of technological and organizational changes and in number of smaller organizations. Also, in early retirements; and
      (iii) Increases in self-employment and in part-time, temporary and contract employment.

Social Security Research Centre, Ahmedabad

(e) Increasing life expectancy.

(f) Increasing cost of education and medical care; and, changing life styles and increasing consumerism that place pressures on income.

Developments

A review of developments relating to provisions for old age and contingencies (referred to as benefits or benefit plans hereafter) in the last about 50 years indicate the following:

1. *Multiple plan approach*

   (a) Three part retirement benefits advocated — provident fund, pension and gratuity. Also medical care plan(s).

   (b) EFPS (1971) and EDLIS (1976) both initiated to provide survivor benefits. And in government and government sector DLIS and savings-cum-insurance scheme.

   (c) Current approach that overlooks nature and extent of coverage is important and not number of plans that may involve overlaps, duplication, different rules and worthwhile avoidable work.

2. *Multiple objectives*

   (a) Provident fund intended to cater to unemployment, for early retirement, superannuation and death or TPD. Also, financial assistance through withdrawals for housing, marriage, illness, life insurance, social/religious obligations etc.; also, settlement upon change of job or after unemployment for two months.

   (b) Liberal withdrawals and settlement procedures contain advantage of compounding, an important ingredient of benefit funds. A review of EPFS reports from 1997 to 1999 indicates the following:

	1997-98	1998-99
Membership as on 31 March (in millions)	17	19
Average balance in EPFS account	Rs. 14, 435	Rs. 16, 891
Average settlement	Rs. 16, 662	Rs. 19, 375
Average withdrawal	Rs. 17, 662	Rs. 20, 207

3. *Segmented approach to legislated benefits*

(a) Legislated benefits are essentially limited to organized sector in specified industries but excluding smaller organizations. After over 45 years of existence membership of EPFS and exempted provident funds (ExPFs) is about 23 million.

(b) Separate legislated plans have been established for coal mines, Assam tea industry and seamen.

(c) A number of welfare funds have been initiated by Central and State Governments as a substitute for EPFO schemes, e.g., employees of construction industry, of beedi industry, for lawyers, craftsmen/technicians, etc. Additionally, Central and many State governments have initiated pension benefits for destitute senior citizens. Also, group insurance plans.

(d) One ESIS review committee suggested seven segment approach that included employees in offices, in plans, in high risk units, etc.

4. *Design of plans*

(a) Final salary type of plans (EPS and gratuity), favor organization/employees with higher salary growth rates. Results in reverse subsidization rather than in cross subsidization, a common feature of a social security program, a feature more essential in a developing economy.

(b) About three fourths of contributions of EPFO schemes and gratuity are used to pay lump sum benefits. Pension accounts for about 6.33 percent of total contributions of over 25 or 29 percent.

(c) Survivor benefit plans are often linked to service, contribution, salary grade, etc., and fails to recognize needs of the family. Illustratively EDLIS links benefit to PF balance; family pension upon death of a government pensioner is linked to salary at retirement.

(d) EFPS and EDLIS benefits have experienced very low claim ratios —— less than one half of interest income at 8.50 percent or less. Notwithstanding mounting surpluses, benefits continued to be modest with very limited improvement.

(e) Major lacunas of EPS are (i) reverse subsidization; (ii) assumes salary growth at 10 per cent without any ceiling, interest at 12 per cent in post-retirement period; (iii) pension commences from age 58 irrespective of NRA; (iv) family pension to a nominee of a deceased employee; (v) fixed factor (Rs.100 for Re.1 of pension) for commutation and refund of capital sum; (vi) pension linked to average salary for the last 12 months with salary including incentives, salary for unutilized leave, lump-sum through a settlement, job linked allowances, etc.; (vii) TPD pension linked to contributory membership and normally less than family pension; (viii) absence of minimum pension for post – EPS members; (ix) discount at 3 per cent, maximum 25 per cent upon early retirement after 50 years of age; (x) member who has not completed contributory membership of 10 years is paid a lump sum etc., etc.

First exemption notification provides for (i) individual account passbook reflecting accretion; (ii) membership of casual, temporary, part time and contract employees; (iii) annual actuarial valuation with employer making up the shortfall, (iv) transfer of account on the basis of balance in the account; and (v) denial for government contribution —EFPS share and to EPS etc., etc.

Individual account and other requirements are totally inconsistent with the basic concept of a benefit defined and especially a final salary type of pension plan and which provides for family and TPD pensions with a minimum, immediate early retirement pension with low discount, and implied indexing.

EPS is designed as if it is an employer plan and not a countrywide plan for organizations in different industries, commercial and service organizations and of different sizes and resources.

(f) In the period April 1995 to March 1999, return of EPS has averages less than 9 per cent as against assumption of 12 per cent. Further, since introduction of the bill in Parliament a number of improvements have been made in EPS including two supplements of 4 per cent each and actuarial reports have not been released.

(g) Plan design is unfair to employees who do not have regular employment and to employees who may work for or in different organization —— casual, temporary, part time and contract employees largely because of principal employer linked membership, qualifying service requirement etc.

(h) PF and gratuity benefit may be better described as deferred remuneration plans rather than as retirement and contingent benefit plans.

5. *Contributions*

(a) High level of contributions to legislated benefit plans of about 33 or 37 per cent fail to provide for indexing of pension, for liberal TPD pension, for unemployment benefit, for minimum pension and provides moderate family pension.

(b) It is now accepted that high contribution rates prompt employers and employees to find ways to contain contributions, and at times to violate legislation.

(c) High contribution rates place pressure on income and accumulations that look large after membership of say 15 years or more make loans and withdrawals unavoidable.

6. *Probability and vesting right*

(a) Benefit defined plans largely preclude portability or are likely to be disadvantageous to the outgoing employee. Deferred pension/benefit concept is also disadvantageous to the outgoing employee as it does not recognize economic changes.

(b) Conservative vesting rights contain pension — 20 years in case of government and government sector employees, and 10 years in EPS even for superannuation. Such conservative vesting rights convert pension/benefit into a reward for long service, contain old age benefits and benefit plans cease to be an integral part of the reward system.

(c) EPFS is fully vested and gratuity vests after five years in case of resignation and termination and is fully vested in case of death and TPD.

7. *Employer plans*

(a) Pension plans —— A large majority of employer sponsored pension plans are limited to management level employees. Some companies limit such plans to managerial levels.

Large majority of the plans are contribution defined pension plans. And, as many companies initiated pension benefits by diverting bonus payment, they are fully vested.

(b) Provident fund and gratuity benefits are provided by almost all organized sector organisations.

(c) Medical assistance — Emphasis is on minor and routine expenses. Medical assistance to retired persons and survivors essentially is limited to some organizations and often to upper level management employees. In such cases benefits are quite liberal.

A number of employers specially smaller organizations limit medical assistance to salary of one month. Public sector organizations are more egalitarian in their approach and many of them provide reasonable to liberal assistance in case of hospitalization and major illnesses.

(d) On the whole, approach of employers may be characterized as elitist and emphasis is on minor illnesses.

8. *Investments*

(a) Regulations essentially limit investments to government securities, government guaranteed/sponsored securities and deposits and to bonds of FIs and PSCs.

Regulations are very detailed with pressure to hold investments to maturity.

(b) Regulations contain income. In some years return was below the inflation rate. And net/real average return of about 2.5 per cent over the last 2 decades has contained accumulations and benefits.

(c) Investments are not well managed in many organisations including EPFO schemes and ESIS. Illustratively, ExPFS did not invest in PSC and FI bonds in first two years of liberalization. Notwithstanding increase in interest coupons till mid 90s and phased liberalization of investment guidelines. EPFS has credited interest at 12 per cent for the last decade.

(d) Better managed benefit funds (PF, gratuity and pension) normally out-perform EPFS and LIC managed benefit funds.

(e) ESIS investment are not well managed and in recent years the return has fluctuated around 6 per cent. As on 31 March 1999, it had invested about 85 per cent of reserves and about 37 per cent of investments were in fixed deposits of banks.

9. *Tax regulations*

(a) Regulations depart from the basic concept of taxation of each income once. Employer contributions and interest are tax exempt in case of provident fund but taxed like income/salary in case of a pension plan.

(b) Regulations are highly discriminatory in favor of employees. The regulations do not include any offset for employers regular contributions upto 35-1/3 per cent of salary to benefit funds. And, dearness relief payments to pensioners are deductible. Reimbursements for minor medical care to an employee up to Rs.15,000 for hospitalization and major medical coverage, for overseas treatment, and for medical care coverage to pensioner and spouse are tax exempt. As against that a self-employed enjoys tax exemption for premium up to Rs. 10,000 for health insurance.

Standard deductions available only in case of employer sponsored pension plans and not for other pension plans.

(c) Regulations do not recognize locked in period.

(d) IT rule 89 requires an approved pension fund to purchase annuities from LIC. However, a recent notification excludes public sector banks and specified FIs from the provision of ITR – 89.

10. *ESIS and CGHS*

(a) Dedicated hospital and dispensary approach results in meaningful under-utilization and precludes extension to smaller location. Limited number of facilities results in higher conveyance expense and loss of time. Specialists are available on specified dates and for a few hours.

(b) Medication is limited to specified list of drugs, and from time to time such drugs are not available at the dispensary or the stores.

(c) Mediclaim plan—Recently initiated age linked premium places older persons at a disadvantage. The changeover results in lower total premium over a period of 75 years as compared to the previous premium rates notwithstanding elimination of sub-limits and increases in fees and costs during about a decade of mediclaim plan. If savings in premium for the highest table of benefits are invested to earn about 8 per cent, accumulation exceeds Rs.1 million, a large enough amount to meet higher age linked claims.

GIS units have adopted one model approach and other proven models have not been considered —— HMO/ managed care, major medicals, comprehensive structure, etc. Also, one premium structure results in insured in smaller locations subsidizing insured in larger and costlier locations.

Emphasis on curative medicine. Periodics de-emphasized. Also, other preventive measures.

Payment from first rupee tends to increase claim ratio and possible misuse. No effort has been made to contain avoidable upgrading and possible misuse through initial deduction, second opinion etc.

Broadly worded exclusions include complaints of which the insured is not aware of. And, technical objections are often made and delays in settlement are common.

11. *Other issues*

(a) Membership – After over 45 years of establishment membership (3/99) of EPFs is 23.12 million and that of ESIS is 9.09 million.

(b) Accumulations—notwithstanding limited membership, premature settlements, withdrawals, etc., investments of EPFO and ESIS controlled schemes including exempted provident funds now exceed Rs.1 trillion.

(c) Regulations — An employer only is permitted to establish benefit funds to make provisions for old age and contingencies for employees of the organization. A common fund for a company and its subsidiaries/affiliates is no longer permitted.

Pension plans of LIC, MFs and others that are open to

any individual are not allowed to issue annuity for life. Employee benefit funds are regulated through IT Act. Naturally, thrust is on tax aspects. And other aspects like governance, disclosures, participation, vesting, accounting, audit and actuarial standards, etc., are ignored.

(d) Design and regulations of legislated plans (EPFO and ESIS) require actions through the principal employer with complex and rigid operating procedures and are not suitable to tiny sector, for persons who do not have regular employment and for self-employed.

(e) LIC—LIC has made limited marketing effort. It has not designed and offered pension plans that are more suitable to bargainable employees and to self-employed. It does not market survivor pension linked to material, age and dependency feature.

Monetary limits on group term insurance policies are low and are limited to death. A level premium term insurance policy is limited to 25 years, insurance amount is limited to Rs. 200,000 and refund of premium approach results in relatively high premium.

Gratuity plans require term insurance feature which increases cost by up to one percent of salary.

Service needs improvements.

These aspects need to be taken into consideration while designing programmes for income security in old age.

10

Pension Market—
New Challenges and Opportunities

H.O.Sonig

The quest for security has been the basic instinct of any human being since time immemorial. This becomes more felt when the individual gets older and his children start ignoring him. The failure of joint family system adds to his woes. It is generally seen that we seldom bother about the oldage provisions in our active life and consequently the heaviest burden we carry in our oldage is our empty purse. The increasing inflation and also uncertainties owing to the peculiar behaviour of the financial market lead to a situation of bewilderment and one is compelled to believe in the value and benefits of pension. There is rightly, therefore, a growing demand for pension from different classes of people. But the market has not been properly tapped. The pension market potential in our country is so vast, but practically not much has been done except the pension provided by the governments, both Central and State, and a few employers here and there. There are, however, reasons for non-development of pension business in India. In our country, pension is compared with the short term investments of Banks and financial institutions by those who have retired with sufficient funds to invest. So far, in our country, the interest rates moved upward for the past so many decades. People, therefore, expect an era of ever increasing interest rates and preffered short term investments. Only recently, the interest rates are experiencing a downward trend. The insurer, on the other hand, can offer non-profit (guaranteed), with profit (with some guarantee) and unit linked (with no guarantee) annuities to the public. The annuities offered, therefore, look unattractive to the people.

When we analyse the reason for non-development of pension market, the following appear to contribute to the same:

- Providing for pensions by saving all through one's working life time necessarily implies availability of long term and relatively safer investment avenues. In our country the long term debt market is not well developed. Equity markets are highly volatile and property is fraught with many legal hurdles.

- Very high inflation rates in the past have discouraged people from sacrificing present consumption for the sake of post-retirement income which may be meager in terms of its purchasing power.
- A further reason for the employers not funding for adequate pension benefit for their employees could be that the limit for tax deductible contribution to be made are defined as percentage of present salaries. In view of high inflation, these limits often turn out to be low in terms of benefit provided as percentage of final salary of the employees.

In chapter IX of the report of the Malhotra Committee on Reforms in Insurance Sector submitted in January 1994 to the Government of India, the Committee has also given the following reasons for insufficient development of Pension provision in our country:

- Availability of other long term savings instruments / provisions such as Employees Provident Fund, Public Provident Fund, Gratuity etc.
- The lumpsum benefits in the form of gratuity and Provident Fund either on death or on retirement looks better alternative in our country.
- In other countries like UK, Canada and the USA etc., the contribution limits for tax incentives are higher. In India the tax relief on contributions to such an extent is not available.
- Unit linked Pension Plans marketed in developed countries by insurance companies have become very popular due to free investment opportunities available to them.
- The tax reliefs to self employed, professionals traders or those employed in the non organized sector on pension provisions are not sufficient.

Retirement Benefits Available in India

Unlike the developed countries, where the pension system is built upon a comprehensive State Pension Provision forming part of the social security net, India does not have any significant State Pension framework for the population as a whole. In fact, it is only the employees in the organized sector who enjoy any kind of retirement benefits. Moreover, until recently, these benefits have been in lump sum form, viz., Provident Fund and Gratuity. As provision of PF and Gratuity is mandatory in case of employers employing a specific number of employees, most of the companies in private sector have traditionally confined their retirement benefit package only to these two benefits. However, most of the government employees are covered under a good DA linked pension scheme.

Occupational pension schemes, traditionally have been few in number, largely focusing on the highly paid managerial staff in private companies.

Pension in Other Countries

Developed countries generally have comprehensive pension systems often built upon a strong social system including State Pension Provision. Most of them have set up schemes whereby the employed and self-employed can save for a certain level of income when they cease active work. Broadly they are of three types labeled as "Three Pillar Concept" by the World Bank. Scheme-wise analysis which may help us understand these systems is as under:

1. Social Security Schemes

These are statutory schemes administered by the governments generally on pay-as-you-go basis. Employers and employees are compulsorily required to contribute to the Social Security Schemes. The main benefit of the Scheme is oldage pension available to individuals after a certain age but there can be other benefits, such as unemployment benefit, sickness benefit, disability benefit etc. The benefit can be a flat amount and /or earning related.

2. Occupational Pension Schemes

Occupational Pension Schemes are set up by employers with contributions from both employers and employees. In some cases the schemes may not require contribution from the employees. Occupational Pension Schemes mainly started as defined benefit schemes, wherein retirement income was assured at a predetermined level in relation to the salary of the employee in the final years of service. Subsequently, defined contribution schemes were adopted by some employers where under the employers liability was limited to making specified contribution to the Scheme and the amount of pension available was determined by the accumulation of the contributions through investments over the years, i.e., the retirement benefit is not guaranteed either in absolute amount or in relation to final salary.

In most of the countries the employers are required to set up irrevocable Trust Funds called Superannuation Funds. The main benefit under and occupational pension scheme is a life annuity for the retiring employee after a predetermined retirement age. The Scheme may also provide equivalent alternative benefits, such as, an annuity guaranteed for certain number of years and thereafter for life (5, 10 or 15 years) or a joint life and last survivor annuity. A portion of the benefits can be taken as a tax free lump sum. Some death-in-service benefits can also be included as a lump sum and/or family pension.

3. Private (Individual) Pension Schemes

Traditionally, insurance companies cater to this need by offering Immediate and Deferred annuity plans. As a result of the desire of the Governments to gradually reduce their social security obligations and encourage private provision for retirement benefits, Governments have encouraged setting up of personal pension systems by appropriate legislation and tax incentives. As regards the benefits, the main benefit can be an annuity payable for life together with option for commutation of a portion of pension for tax free lump sum as in the case of occupational pension schemes Subsequently changes have come about by which the participants were given a choice to defer the pension vesting age and in the meanwhile allowed to take "income withdrawls".

The Scene in India and Asia

In our country so far most of the retirement benefits have been lump sum in two forms: Provident Fund and Gratuity. We have a very large Employees Provident Fund Organisation covering around 3 lakh establishments and 2.15 crore employees. The employees Pension Scheme 1995 has done a lot to popularize the concept of pension. The scheme effective from 16th November 1995 is being administered through Central Provident Fund Commissioner. All employees covered under Employees Provident Fund and Miscellaneous Provisions Act, 1952 are eligible for this scheme. Employers contributions to the provident fund are restricted to 8.33 per cent of the employees pay not exceeding Rs.5000 per month plus 1.16 per cent of the employees pay is contributed by the Central Government for attractive benefits. As in India, Provident Funds are an accepted form of employee benefits in Malayasia and Singapore.

Benefits of the Pension Funds to the Economy

Direct Benefits

The most obvious benefit of a pension fund for the society is provision of financial security in oldage. Today, with ageing of the population being worldwide problem addressing the needs of the older generation has become a major concern of the governments and the societies at large. Funded pension and other related post retirement benefits relieve the earning people of the insecurity of a penurious retirement and thus contribute to the overall welfare of the society.

Indirect Benefits

1. **Development of the Capital market:** In developed countries like UK, equities are considered to be the most ideal investment for funds backing the pension liabilities. This is for two reasons:

(a) the liabilities are payable over a long term, and
(b) they are of 'real' type, i.e., their amounts generally increase with salary inflation, which has a close link with economic growth in turn, with returns on equity shares.

In the developed economies pension funds are the biggest investors in the stock market.

Similarly, when trying to match their fixed monetary liabilities they also invest huge amounts in the long term Government and corporate bonds. Thus, by providing a boost to the capital market pension funds promote capital formation and economic development.

2. **Property Market:** Real estate, especially commercial property, is another major avenue of long term real investment favoured by pension funds. They buy or construct office blocks, factories, shopping complexes, etc. on freehold or long lease and try to earn a growing but stable rental income, as a means to diversify

their investments from equities. Thus, these funds contribute very significantly to industrial and commercial progress.

3. Infrastructure Devlopment: Pension funds can invest heavily in infrastructure due to availability of large long term funds at their disposal. Infrastructural development has to be provided faster than what it is today. Any economic growth is connected with this development. Infrastructure projects are essentially long term ventures. The yield is expected after certain gestation period. Long term funds are therefore required for such projects These could be ideally provided by pension sector. The Rakesh Mohan Committee Report on Infrastructure suggests that a very heavy fund is required over the next decade to promote this sector, which can be taken care of by Insurance and Pension sectors. Thus by developing pension segment and annuity funds, we can certainly contribute towards the development of our county's economy.

4. Maturing of Financial Sector: By mobilizing vast investible resources for people, the pension schemes can:

- Improve the overall saving rate of the economy,
- Give impetus to development of new investment media, like gold bonds, index linked bonds, money market instruments, gilt –strips etc., and
- Contribute to the overall deepening and widening of the financial markets.

Need for Pension Reform

Before we discuss this, let us see what we should try to achieve through reform, or what are the characteristics of a good pension system.

Basically, the system should seek to strike a balance among the following diverse aims:

- Providing a reasonably adequate level of post-retirement income for all in the country;
- Ensuring security of promised retired benefits;
- Minimizing the cost of such provision by;

(a) having a simple cost effective administrative mechanism,
(b) a not too onerous regulatory system,

(c) maximizing the return on funds invested till benefits become payable.

- Making the system flexible, visible and seif-sustaining in the long run; and
- Promoting saving, capital formation and economic development.

Pension Structure

Generally, a comprehensive pension structure for a country consists of provisions of retirement income and other retirement benefits (e.g., lump sum on retirement, post-retirement health care, benefits for dependants, etc.) at the three levels mentioned earlier. Hence, while devising a three tier pension framework as outlined above for India, it would be advisable to examine the experience of some of the developed countries of Europe and North America and also the recent attempts made by newly emerging economies of Asia, East Europe and Latin America.; the objective should be to learn from their mistakes and to acquire those aspects of their systems which have weathered the test of time successfully.

The biggest problem faced by the government in West European countries to-day is the increasing unsustainability of the present largely unfounded State pensions. As the human longevity continues to improve at an accelerating pace and birth rates continue to fall in these countries, the shrinking number of people in the income earning age relative to the number of pensioners implied a rapidly rising tax burden being imposed on existing workforce to meet the increasing benefits to those who have retired. The mounting resistance of working population to bear this burden and the social frictions arising from such inter generational inequality is compelling these Governments to widely debate these issues, and to consider the alternative of funded predominantly private pension arrangements in place of the existing PAYG State Pension Schemes.

Secondly, some of the countries like UK, which have evolved a comprehensive and elaborate regulatory and tax system to ensure security of retirement benefits at all the three levels are also realizing the adverse impact which excessive regulations might be having on the market forces governing the pension sector.

Russia's pension system is also in trouble, as its 38.5 million retired workers have been among the hardest hit by the country's chaotic post-Soviet economic and social regression. The State-run

Pension Fund is financed by active workers, a system being questioned in most countries, due to the growing financial burden of an ageing population. Employers contribute 28 per cent of the salary, while employees add one percent.

Thus we must be careful to avoid the pitfalls while evolving our own system.

Recommendations for Reform

When we talk of reform, the first question that arises is reform by whom?

While it is true that the various entities involved in the pension provision, viz., the individual buyers of pension products, corporate sponsors and the Government as a sponsor behave in response to the market forces, the initial stimulus for these forces to evolve and develop must come from the government.

The government measures can basically take two forms:

(a) A comprehensive Act, supported by Rules and regulations to be enforced by a Regulatory Authority; and
(b) An effective but simple system of tax incentives to promote the pension development.

Regulatory Mechanism

So far in our country, there is no formal regulatory authority nor a separate law to regulate the pension market. However, an encouraging development is the setting up of the Insurance Regulatory and Development Authority (IRDA) and the measures contemplated by this Authority for future enforcement. These measures include development of the concept of Appointed Actuary for Insurance Companies (which sell pension products among others) and the Group Pension Schemes. The Appointed Authority regulation makes it compulsory for all the schemes and insurers to appoint an Actuary, who will have statutory responsibility to ensure, as far a s possible, the management of these companies and schemes on sound financial lines. The objective will be to maximize the probability of these institutions fulfilling their promises to the beneficiaries. The actuary will advise these schemes on designing and pricing of financially viable products, maintenance of adequate resources, sound investment of funds and allocation of surpluses etc. among different beneficiary groups.

Tax Reforms

In our country, tax incentives and conditions imposed by the tax authorities for availing these incentives have been the major driving force shaping the retirement benefit structure. These can continue to be so, provided they are aligned suitably to th other regulatory measures.

Some of the modifications which are suggested to promote growth of pension culture are;

i. Defining the contributions towards occupational pension schemes in terms of what is needed to provide the desired (defined) benefits as proportion of final salaries and not as a proportion of present salaries. This will enable the employers to fund for adequate final benefits without sacrificing tax concessions;
ii. Reducing the proportion of commuted pension so as to provide adequate security in older ages;
iii. Designing an attractive system of tax incentives for private pensions; and
iv. Specifying limit for all benefits, which are linked to an appropriate inflation index, and so on.

Regulation of Market Practices

Another important component of regulation is regulation of market practices of pension and other service providers so that the people are not lured into paying for benefits that are not suited to their needs. This is indeed a very tricky area. It is very difficult to draw a dividing line between information and misinformation, between freedom and license. The market is in the long term its own regulator It throws the unscrupulous players out. However, that may take years. In short, the public must be protected against misleading publicity and unfair practices.

The Regulatory Authority

Finally, to integrate the various regulatory measures into a comprehensive framework, a Regulatory Authority will have to play its role. The authority must however, enforce its rules as far as possible not by centralising all its functions but by delegating them to the professional bodies like those of Auditors, Actuaries, Investment

Managers, etc. so as to allow the professional's expertise and integrity to take care of public interest.

The government is examining to draw up the legal framework for planing the regulation of Pensions under IRDA to regulate the Pension Funds market under the umbrella of the IRDA. Now when the Insurance Sector is open, the massive domestic pension market may be well developed. The Dave Committee report on devising a pension system for the country has recommended a system for private sector management of pension funds with the idea of generating market linked returns instead of a fixed rate of return under the current system. As mentioned above, the pension market in India has yet to develop. According to the Dave Committee report, six professional pension fund managers should be selected to manage the retirement funds under the system. Each will offer three schemes or styles – namely, safety first, balanced income and high growth. The system suggested is slightly similar to that based on Chilean model. Both are fully funded Individuals pay for their accumulations and pensions. Both rely on private professional managers for fund management and a competitive offering for annuities. The scheme will offer wider choice and scope for maximizing returns during young age and minimization of risk as people become older.

The growth in agriculture, recovery of industrial production and creation of fresh demand have influenced the economic growth of the country in a brighter way. The Government is taking steps to improve economic activities and attract foreign investments to herald a better outlook for the year 2000-2001. Infrastructure appears to hold the key for accelerating economic take off. In such a scenario and in the context of developing economy, it is very difficult for anybody to maintain the same standard of living in oldage.

In India while the total population between the year 1991 and 2016 is expected to rise by 49 per cent (from 846.7 million to 1263.5 million) the number of aged (60 and above) is expected to increase by 107 per cent during the same period. The pension market has, therefore, to address the issues of social adequacy and equity. To achieve this objective is a formidable challenge. However, there is no single recipe for pension reforms. The details like design, regulation and implementation will make substantial difference to the final outcome. Undue delay and inaction in the face of unsustainable pension system may put the country at a disadvantageous position in the competitive market.

We can also learn from others' mistakes. The first step is to liberalise portfolio allocation rules. The second step is to provide for an increased role for private pension management; following the examples of countries like Chile may produce better results. The third step is to create an awareness among the public to avoid oldage crisis in future.

As we approach the era of rapid changes in the economic and social environment the pension market will provide financial security. New players of insurance will have a deeper study of the market and will intensify their activities to reach out to the masses through their innovative marketing methods and attractive pension products so that the flame of oldage security burns bright even in the humblest of homes.

11

Health Security and Long Term Care Principles and Practices

DR. A.K. KHOKAR*

"Ageing is not a disease but a normal part of the life process"

Ageing is inevitable and irreversible but does not automatically lead to ill health. Many of the health conditions associated with ageing can be prevented or delayed if people have access to decent living conditions and suitable health care throughout their lives.

The people in age group 60 and above are considered as elderly and are termed as aged. The single most obvious indication of ageing is the change in the condition of the skin which tends to dry and wrinkle. In addition, the person's capacity for sight and hearing is reduced gradually, the brain begins to shrink, losing 100,000 cells per day, the muscles become weaker, joints stiffen and swell, the heart, lungs, bladder and kidneys begin to operate at reduced levels of efficiency and the output of hormones diminishes. The body becomes increasingly susceptible to stress, infection, and degenerative processes. Most of the people develop feelings of loneliness, boredom, and. loss of self esteem.

The problems suffered by the aged are generally security oriented—general security, income security, emotional security and health security.

The aged are prone to various diseases which occur mainly at the age of 60+.

They are:

- Degenerative changes,
- Arteriosclerosis and ischemic heart diseases,
- Prostate enlargement,
- Kidney diseases,
- Cancer,
- Joint diseases,
- Gout,

*Deputy Medical Commissioner, ESIC Corporation

- Diabetes,
- Senile dementia,
- Cataract,
- Glaucoma,
- Chronic constipation,
- Elderly get sleep with difficulty and wake up quickly. They are mostly drowsy and do not sleep well,
- Sensory impairments lead to chances of accidents Serious consequences occur; mobility declines,
- Neglect and abuse of the elderly is a common feature. Research suggests that elder abuse is well-spread, occurs amongst all sub-groups of the population and affects 4 to 10 per cent of the aged people, and
- Dementia, delirium, loneliness, substance abuse, social isolation, lack of housing or proper environment are the common problems of the aged.

One of the major issues which requires urgent attention is the need to provide medical services at primary, secondary and tertiary levels including terminal care.

Geriatric Medicine

Geriatric medicine is an approach to general medical care of the elderly and is concerned with the clinical preventive, remedial and social aspects of illness of the elderly. The basic principles of geriatric medicine include:

- Knowledge specific to health care of elderly,
- Knowledge specific to medical care of the elderly,
- Understanding that older people are likely to suffer more of the side effects of medication,
- Latrogenic illness is a constant threat, and
- Knowledge, that coordinated care is needed to appreciate and to fully mobilize social, familial, financial and psychological support.

National Policy for the Older Persons

The National Policy assures the older persons that their concerns are the national concern and it aims to secure a legitimate place to the older persons in society. The policy visualizes that the State will extend support in the areas of :

- Financial security;
- Health care;
- Shelter;
- Welfare;
- Protection against abuse and exploitation; and
- Provision of opportunities for development of older persons potential.

With regard to health care, the Policy lays down the following guidelines:

(a) There should be a judicial mix of public health services, health insurance and health services provided by non-profit organizations and private medical care.

(b) Provision of geriatric services at primary secondary and tertiary levels with appropriate public sector outlays and proper distribution of services in urban and rural areas.

(c) The development of health insurance to be given high priority to cater to the needs of different income segments.

(d) Private general practitioners should be given orientation in geriatric care.

(e) It should be ensured that geriatric patients are not required to wait for long or to make repeated visits.

(f) Trusts, charitable societies, voluntary agencies should be offered grants, tax relief and allotment of land at concessional rates to encourage them to provide free treatment to poor elderly population, including free beds medicines and diet.

(g) Medical and para medical staff should be given training and orientation in the health-care of the elderly. Training in nursing should include geriatric care.

(h) Mobile health services, camps and ambulance services should be provided.

(i) Hospitals should be encouraged to have separate welfare funds for service to the elderly by collecting donations.

(j) Hospices should be set up to cater to the needs of persons who have been abandoned without any family support and those who are chronically ill and are admitted to public hospitals.

(k) Easy to follow guidance materials on health and nursing care of older persons should be prepared and distributed for the use of family care givers.

(l) Preventive health and health education programmes should be strengthened.

(m) Mental health services and provision of counseling services to care-givers of older persons should be strengthened.

(n) NGOs should be encouraged and assisted to provide ambulatory services, day care and health care to supplement the efforts of the State.

Status of Health Care Services of the Elderly

Health services are available to the elderly as per the packages drawn up under the various medical schemes. Thus within the government sector, the aged are provided services through a network of health centres, dispensaries, and hospitals along with other beneficiaries.

The important services provided to the elderly through governmental or non-governmental health institutions include:

- Preferential treatment is provided to the elderly at the OPD Diagnostic facilities, X-ray and laboratories through separate queues.
- Ambulances are made available for transportation of the elderly sick persons.
- Professional nurses visit homes for home care of the elderly.
- Day care is provided as an alternative to institutionalization.
- Geriatric clinics are set up in many hospitals and health centres on specific days and at specific times.
- Hospices are available in some community settings for the care of the terminally ill persons.
- Mobile health care facilities for diagnosis and treatment are provided at specified places and specified timings.
- Counselling is available on health issues through various health institutions and societies.
- Publicity materials explaining the various health problems and how to deal with them are made available through various agencies and institutions.
- Special camps are organized to perform cataract operations within the hospitals and community settings.
- A number of outdoor clinics have been set up for early diagnosis of cancer.
- A number of community programmes and services are

available to help people maintain independence through

(a) senior citizen centres,
(b) nutritional services,
(c) meal delivery services,
(d) telephone services,
(e) transport and escort services,
(f) emergency response services, and
(h) subsidized trips to historical and religious places.

Health Security for the Elderly under the ESI Scheme

Under the ESI Scheme, the following categories of the aged are provided with services:

(a) Dependent parents of insured person.
(b) Insured persons and their spouses after superannuation on payment of a nominal contribution of Rs.10 per month.
(c) Retired employees of the ESI Corporation.

The scale of medical benefit is comprehensive and includes:

Outpatient treatment,
Domiciliary treatment,
In patient treatment,
Specialist consultation,
Free supply of drugs and dressings aids and appliances,
Diagnostic facilities,
Super specialty services,
Ambulance services,
Services under various National Health Programmes.
Separate queues for the aged, preferential treatment at diagnostic facilities, organization of special campaigns for screening of chronic diseases, counselling, mental health services etc. are available in some ESI institutions.

Keeping in view the National Policy for the Older Persons the following action is being planned :

- Organisation of preferential treatment for the elderly at dispensaries, diagnostic centres and hospitals.
- Regular geriatric clinics at dispensaries and hospitals.
- Strengthening of domiciliary services for the aged.
- Provision of special ambulance facilities for the aged.
- Development of ISM facilities within the existing institutions to cater to the needs of the needs of the aged.

- Organisation of special campaigns and camps to deal with specific problems of the aged.
- Reservation of beds for the aged in each ESI Hospital.
- Publication of IEC materials for the aged.
- Training and CME programmes for medical nursing and paramedical staff to deal with the aged.
- Organisation of various health education activities through special disease detection camps, public lectures, exhibitions, films etc.

Development of Resources and Services for the Long Term Care of the Aged

Discussion so far has focused on the problems of the young aged (60-75). People are generally active in this age group and mainly need social adjustment. The problems of the old aged (75+) need careful planning. Many of the old aged have mobility restrictions, dementia, medical problems and need assistance. As far as possible, older persons should be cared for in community and family settings. This approach provides quality care and is certainly less expensive than institutional alternatives. There is now an emerging consensus for a more holistic approach incorporating the assessment of physical and social conditions as well as the economic and environmental factors.

The decisions regarding allocation of resources and planning of services for the old-aged should be undertaken in a decentralized manner, separately for each local area, as per national guidelines keeping in view the growth of the aged population, the cultural norms and value systems in the respective areas. In particular, the services should be planned according to the physical and mental status of the aged people as follows:

(1) Household and Personal Care,

  Unimpaired,
  Impaired with minor handicap,
  Appreciable severe handicap, and
  Very serious handicap.

(2) Mobility

  No difficulty,
  Can get out of house with assistance, and
  Housebound but can get around the house
  Chair-fast or bed-fast.

(3) Mental State
Normal,
Mild dementia,
Moderate or severe dementia.

(4) Physical Environment
Good Housing with easy access to hot water inside WC etc,
Poor housing with difficult access to both.

(5) Social Environment
Living alone,
Living with spouse,
Living with others.

In view of the limited resources and depending on the needs of the individuals, the following options may be considered:

- Hospitals — Psychiatric, Geriatric,
- Residential homes,
- Special housing,
- Day care centres,
- Day centre visits plus home helps, home nursing, home meals,
- Ordinary housing with availability of static /mobile medical facilities.

Although long term care costs for the elderly will rise considerably with ageing population, the burden will not be unsustainable. In the coming decade, the major challenges for the health policy makers will be to evolve strategies for community based services with beneficiary participation in planning and choosing the services. The prerequisites for any such planning are:

(a) Universality of Health Coverage: To ensure cost effective programme strategies will have to be evolved to coordinate services for elderly through the network of primary health centres.

(b) Equity: There is need to strike a right balance between public support and individual responsibility. This requires appropriate income security programme for the elderly.

(c) Quality: Assuring quality services requires practical measures that can assess the performance of the entire system in maintaining independence and functional status.

(d) Integration: Merging of medical care and long term care for the elderly requires various models to serve a wider population and coordinate early medical and social interventions to promote maximum effectiveness.

(e) Supporting informal care giving: Policy makers must find ways to relieve and support overburdened care-givers while avoiding incentives to shift care unnecessarily to the formal sector.

(f) Promote healthy ageing: Prevention is the key word. Though many chronic illnesses are not preventable still their debilitating effects can be reduced through secondary prevention and rehabilitation. Closer integration of health and social services is essential to achieving the goal.

Conclusion

The aged people in any society represent a storehouse of knowledge and experience and a reservoir of wisdom. Their knowledge and wisdom should be tapped in the national interest. But that cannot be done unless their problems are addressed. The problems of the aged require an in depth study, analysis and research. In our country unfortunately, the population explosion is so devastating that in the national agenda the problems of the senior citizens have been relegated to the background. They should be given due priority. The National Policy for the Older Persons which has identified the problems of the elderly as well as the solutions thereto should be translated into reality through appropriate action plans and financial allocations, and cost effective programmes should be drawn up for their welfare. Among these, programmes of health care and long term care of the elderly should be given high priority.

12

Psychological Security for Older Persons in India

DR INDIRA JAI PRAKASH*

The growing number of older people in the population has resulted in an increased concern with the issue of social security. Developing countries face several problems in managing a large segment of dependent elderly. Inadequate resources, lack of preparation on the part of the government agencies combined with sweeping social changes are responsible for this concern. Societies need to provide a life that is comfortable and dignified to the elderly. The quest to maintain quality of life of older persons usually focuses on economic security. However it is well recognized that health and emotional security are as important as economic security.

The ingredients of psychological security could be broken down to some important components. People, as they age, need to feel wanted, feel useful, have autonomy and feel that their opinion are valued and respected. In the anthropological and sociological literature, women and men at various points in their life course are reported as moving into new and different statuses. In pre-industrial societies midlife and elderly status typically opened up a series of roles generally reserved to those of advanced years and those roles conferred prestige. People caught inadvertently in the path of modernization, may find that activities associated with certain valued roles are no longer open to them.

In traditional societies, old people were valued for their wisdom, their understanding of the nature, and their experience in the agricultural business. They were the repositories of tradition and took care of moral education of the young. They were the healers caring for the sick of the community. Their authority and prestige stemmed from the fact that they had survived the ravages of time affectively. In rural areas, older people who control the family property exercise

* Professor of Psychology and Director, Adult/Population Education Resource Centre, Bangalore University, Bangalore.

power over the youngsters. Religious rituals, initiation rites, decisions regarding issues of importance to kin group or community are the domain of older people. Often the culture of a group is transmitted by word of mouth from generation to generation. A shift from a predominantly agrarian society could lead to a decline in the status of the aged. The aged lose power over others by losing control over the land; they cannot compete with younger persons in technological and non-agricultural occupations, moving from village to city weakens the influence of the old on the young and changing technology and social structure tend to make the aged old fashioned and obsolete (Chaney, 1989).

Traditional Indian society had structured the life cycle of its people in such a way that old people experienced psychological security. There was a gradual movement from active, family oriented life to more withdrawn life style given to spiritual pursuits. It was mandatory for the younger to respect the older and honour their opinions. The joint family system provided the necessary economic and social security. Presence of children and grandchildren and the position as the senior most person in the family supplied them with a sense of satisfaction and pride. Social scientists notice that there is a drastic change in the family and community at present. These changes will imply a different philosophy of life and inter- actional pattern among generations. Age based status (that is 'Ascribed') in our society is giving way to function based (that is, 'Achieved') status which is a common value in industrial societies.

Even in traditional societies, factors external to family system were needed to ensure that the aged were treated well. The most important among these factors which reinforced the ability of the family to provide a caring environment for the aged was the 'community'. This community, variously known as 'biradri', caste or kin groups or sect, constituted a social institution that defined and laid down the moral sanctions for the care of the aged., weak, handicapped, and widowed. The moral sanctions were dynamic and continued to change with changes in economy, ecology and demographic structure of the society (Singh, 1996). Joint family system had the motto "from each according to his/her ability, to each according to his/her need" (Nayar, 1996). This covered not only the old, but others in need like widows, physically handicapped and chronically ill. Family system with its extended structure had a large measure of stability and the old person had a secure position in it.

Community also exerted pressure by close scrutiny and in exceptional cases would take over the care of the disadvantaged. Such a system assured status, honour and security to the aged.

Manifestations of Psychological Insecurity in the Aged

In oldage, it is not enough if one is economically secure. A person may still feel threatened and helpless due to a variety of reasons. Emotional insecurity may express itself in the form of loneliness, lowered life expectation, feeling of powerlessness and depression.

Loneliness and well-being: A great deal of gerontological literature has accumulated regarding correlates and predictors of life satisfaction. Very often the term 'Emotional Well Being' is used interchangeably with the term life satisfaction. There is sufficient evidence in literature to indicate that loneliness is negatively related to life satisfaction. Social interaction and loneliness are crucial factors in the lives of older persons. Studies show that family plays a crucial role in social integration of the old. Family is their major source of social interaction. Older people usually pick their spouse as the confidant. Having a confidant with whom one can share feelings is considered essential for fighting off loneliness in oldage. A factor that is closely related to loneliness is the health status of the person.

Elderly persons with poor health tend to have fewer contacts with others. Their social network shrinks due to disability. Problems with vision and mobility are the two common causes that lead to social isolation of the aged. Since age increases the probability of losing a spouse the problem worsens. Old people are in an unenviable position of losing a confidant as well as not being able to replace lost relationships with new friendship network. There is also a trend for older persons to restrict their social interactions to their immediate family or neighbourhood. They also pick friends from among people with similar characteristics. This trend further narrows down the choices available to older people for interaction. Smaller families, loss of spouse, poor health, death of peers leave the aged with a growing sense of loneliness. There is clear evidence that loneliness is a critical correlate of life satisfaction(Anuradha & Prakash,1991). Old people who are active and who have better social network report less loneliness and more life satisfaction. There is a gender angle to this result that needs to be highlighted. In general, more men than women reported having friends and confidants. They had higher life satisfaction and lesser feelings of loneliness. The reason for this trend was most women as they age lose their spouse. In the 60+ age group, there are disproportionately more widows than widowers (Prakash, 1999). Women who are designated as old now are less likely to have moved freely in the community. They were more house bound and had little opportunity to take active part in occupational and community activities. Hence, with age, they lose whatever limited social networks they had.

Loneliness threatens the elderly both in the developed and developing countries. In cities, many affluent elderly are living alone. They are economically secure but are burdened with a sense of loneliness. Urban older women constitute a large group living alone. Most widowed women in urban areas opt to live by themselves. This trend may be due to their relatively more secure economic position. And the dislike to migrate to a strange place in oldage along with the children. Such living arrangements will have long term consequences. Living arrangements of people determine their quality of life. Availability of help, amount of support, frequency of support, emergency help and long term care depend on where the elders live (Prakash, 1999). Living alone in oldage will make older women much more vulnerable. Older people who are institutionalized feel the loneliness much more acutely. In India, oldage homes are not a popular option yet. Most of the homes for the aged run on charity. Another class of homes are for the relatively well to do, who pay for their upkeep. Self-confidence, independence, and self-reliance are the major casualties of advancing age. In institutions, problems such as sadness, helplessness and feelings of worthlessness are common among inmates. Women suffer more from feeling of sadness, while men report more loneliness. The major reason for institutionalization in our society is lack of family support (Pinto, 1991). The opportunity for varied types of social interaction is much more when the older people live in families. Institutionalised elderly feel deprived of the family support and solicitude and thus feel lonely. In a series of recent studies (Prakash, 2003) urban middle and upper middle class older people living alone reported unhappiness due to absence of children. Parents of non-resident Indians who did not wish to migrate felt the burden of loneliness though economically secure.

Life Satisfaction in Older People

There is close relationship between age and life satisfaction. In oldage, poor health, exit events, (such as death of spouse, loss of jobs etc.) and reduced social interaction are cited as causes of lowering life satisfaction. Most Indian studies report women to be lower on life satisfaction than men at all ages (Prakash, 1994, 1995). A problem with activities of daily living (ADL) is strongly correlated with poor life satisfaction (Prakash, 1997). There is a very strong relationship between self-rated health and life satisfaction. Income is also a variable, though its effect becomes smaller when other factors are controlled (Sreenivas 1999). Apart from loneliness, frequency of worrying, perceived uselessness, lack of happiness affect life satisfaction (Patil et al, 1991). Urban and rural elderly report different levels of life satisfaction due to economic reasons. Marital status and social status are two other factors related to life satisfaction. Adjustment to the ageing process is determined by the amount of satisfaction people have with their present life. Also when goals one had set for oneself are perceived as unfulfilled, felt unhappiness is greater (Ramamurthi 1997). Satisfaction with life is one of the markers of 'successful aging' along with flexibility and good coping. Lowered life satisfaction is a consequence of unsatisfactory living arrangements. Many older women complain that caring for an older spouse and lack of careers for their personal needs make them unhappy (Prakash, 2003).

Depression in Oldage

Depression is perhaps the strongest evidence for lack of emotional security at any age. The elderly form a high risk group for depression apart from other psychiatric symptoms. In India, depression is found to form the bulk of total mental morbidity in the oldage (Rao, 1997). Similarly, elderly form a high risk group for suicide. The suicide rates rise sharply from the young -old to old-old. Physical diseases of painful and incurable nature are not the only cause for such depression. Fall in self-esteem, sense of hopelessness, discrimination and enduring poverty, make a person to contemplate suicide.

Depressive mood state, if not full blown clinical syndrome, is also much more common in oldage. Women report much more such symptoms than men (Prakash, 1989). Mild depression in the form of feeling despondent, discouraged, worried is fairly common. Lack of family and social integration is responsible for such feelings. It was also found that aged who do not have a fixed residence, who have restrictions on their movement, those who had lost their dear ones and who had poor social contacts, experienced greater depression (Bhogle & Reddy). Studies of institutionalized elderly report greater depressive feelings in the residents (Dhillon & Samat, 1992). Not having friends, not being able to structure their time, smaller social network contributed to these feelings. These depressive symptoms include feelings of loneliness and hopelessness. These findings reinforce the belief that family is perhaps the greatest source of emotional security in oldage.

Status and Perceived Sense of Control

Old people need love, respect and need to feel important more than anything else. Nayar (1997) found that even in relatively well to do, elderly people in Kerala felt emotionally insecure because they did not feel cared for or respected. Old people feel that the young should listen to them, ask their opinion and consult them in matters of importance or else they feel redundant.

In any society status of a person is determined by the role and authority held by the person. Roles vary according to age, sex and structural positions. Status and authority are sometimes lost, relinquished or taken over. Under normal circumstances, changes in status and roles are slow and gradual. Individuals may retain some roles and status that are advisory and supervisory in nature as they grow older. Earlier, a man in his prime used to wield authority and power in his family. He (usually it used to be a man)would control both human and material resources which provided emotional security. This sense is drastically changing. Surveying several rural communities Gurumurthy (1991) reports that old people no longer are the masters they once were. They would be happy if they are at least treated as guests in their families.

Ageism, a term coined by Butler (1975) refers to discrimination directed toward old people. In the present social context, old people may feel powerless because of the negative attitude of the younger people, Sweeping technological changes also make adjustment difficult as the environment becomes strange and complex Dependence on the younger family members is also very high due to health and economic reasons. These reduce the perceived sense of power in old people. There is also a trend for perceiving older people as burden on the state economy. These factors lead to a feeling of powerlessness in the elderly.

A more dangerous aspect of such powerlessness is the possibility of abuse of elders. Elder abuse is considered to be on the rise in recent years. Old people who are dependent on care-givers may be neglected due to the caring burden they impose on care-givers or, their helplessness may be financially exploited by others. It may lead to depriving the old for even their basic needs, neglect of their welfare for even active abuse. This may go unnoticed as well as unreported most of the time. In India, in recent years, elder abuse is emerging as an issue (Prakash, 2003).

Relation between Social and Emotional Security

Social or economic security is closely related to emotional or psychological security. All said and done, economic condition does make a difference to happiness. Quality of life is determined by health as well as social and economic status. Health itself is a multifaceted phenomena influenced by socio-economic factors. Economic dependency is a major factor that causes depression in oldage. It is often most distressing to the aged that they have to depend for their needs on younger family members who may resent the expenses incurred on health care needs of the old. This feeling is much more pronounced in older women. Women in oldage become totally dependent on family members in the absence of their own income. (Prakash, 1999).

Compared to younger age groups, older clearly have lower incomes (Bali, 1997). Significant differences exist even among the elderly themselves. Many find that after their retirement, their economic level gets lowered drastically. Even salaried people become economically insecure after retirement. The insecurity is related to lowered life satisfaction and morale. The problems are much more serious in unorganized sector (Mohanty, 1996). Vijay Kumar reports that most older people tend to have little or no accumulated savings. This influences their ability to negotiate with the family. Their lowered status and feelings of helplessness are sometimes the offshoot of the inadequacy. The problems of aged become more acute due to poverty.

Personal autonomy is one of the indicators of quality of life in oldage and this personal autonomy is achieved through a delicate balance of physical, economical and psychological factors (Vijay Kumar, 1997). This balance is easily disrupted in oldage. Illness, inadequate housing, poor income, insufficient social support and inaccessible public services lead to dependency in oldage. Nearly 80 per cent of the aged lose their leading status and control over their families. 85 per cent of rural aged are unable to maintain even optimum standards of food, clothing, housing and other social amenities.

The social security cover for elderly in India is pretty limited and is unlikely to become totally comprehensive in the near future. The oldage pension scheme does not cover all those who really need it. It appears that under the present circumstances, family system still offers better social security to the aged. This security involves not only socio-economical, but also psycho-emotional security. There is still some type of familism in India, which needs to be strengthened. The culture promotes the idea that older people should be cared for (Prakash, 2002). But families' ability to care for elderly is diminishing. Our efforts should be aimed at improving families' inclination. Families need financial help, support in long term care and improved social facilities so that they are not unduly stressed. Some sort of comprehensive social security that covers the economic and health needs of the elderly would take the burden off the families. There will be less dependence on the part of the older, resulting in a feeling of control. Intergenerational relations will also improve as the morale of elderly.

It is clear that mere economic security will not solve the emotional vacuum that older people experience. Organising them in self-help groups, promoting social activity among them, involving them more closely in community work will help provide them the much needed psychological security. Intergenerational understanding has to be actively promoted to remove the negative attitudes young have towards the old. Old also need to change their mindset and learn to adjust to changing times to maintain harmonious relations with the young. Economic security puts bread on the table. Psychological security adds the flavour and taste to that bread. Family community and society should work with the government to ensure total security to older people.

References

Anuradha, B.R. and Prakash I.J., (1991), Life Satisfaction in Relation to Social Interaction and Loneliness among the elderly, in Prakash I.J., Quality of Aging : Collected papers, Varanasi Association of Gerontology, India, pp 151-157

Bhogle, S and Reddy, R, (1996), Depression and Family Jointedness among the Aged; in V.Kumar (ed) *Aging: Indian Perspective and Global Scenario*, New Delhi, AIIMS, pp 178-181.

Bali, R.N., (1975), Psychiatry and Psychology of the Middle Aged; in Freedman, A.M., Kaplan, H.J & Saddock, B.J. (ed): *Comprehensive Text book of Psychiatry II Vol 2*, Baltimore, Williams & Williams.

Chaney E.M., (1984), Empowerment of Older women; Evidence form Historical and Contemporary Sources; in AARP & IFA Document; Empowering Older women; Cross Cultural Views, AARP.

Dhillon, P.K., Samat, S, (1992), Emotional States on the Institutionalised Aged; in Dhillon, P.K.(Ed) *Psychosocial Aspects of Aging in India*, New Delhi, Concept pp 215-240.

Gurumurthy, K.G., (1991), Guests or masters? Changing Status and Authority of Aged; in Rural Karnataka; in Prakash I.J. (ed) Quality Aging—Collected Papers, Varanasi Association of Gerontology, India pp 113-123.

Gurumurthy K.G., (1998), *The Aged in India*, New Delhi, Reliance.

Mohanty M., (1996), Bio-Social Study of Aged People in Orissa; in V.Kumar (ed) *Aging Indian Perspective and Global Scenario*, New Delhi, AIIMS, pp 136-141.

Nayar, P.K.B., (1997), The elderly in India; their Problems and Needs, *Bold* 6(2), pp 2-8.

Nayar P.K.B., (1997), Meeting the challenges of an aging population in Kerala: A suggested Policy and Plan of Action, *Bold* 7(3), pp 11-15.

Prakash I.J., (1989), Life Cycle Changes in Aging Indian Women: Career Award Project Report, New Delhi, University Grants Commission.

Prakash I.J., (1994), Gender Aging; Psychosocial issues; in Ramachandra C.R and Shah B.(ed) *Public Health Implication of Population Aging*, New Delhi, ICMR, pp 24-29.

Prakash I.J., (1995), Family and Mental health of the elderly –Some Emerging Issues, *Indian Journal of Social Psychology*, 11(1), pp 26-29.

Prakash I.J., (1996), Aging Women: A Liability or an Asset? *Research and Development Journal*, 2(2), pp 28-32.

Prakash I.J., (1997), The Status and Conditions of Elderly Widows in India; in Bagchi, K. (ed) *Elderly Females in India—Their Status and Suffering*, New Delhi SGR, and Helpage India, pp 45-64.

Prakash I.J., Living Arrangements of the Elderly in India; Implications for Care Giving, Aging and Society, *Indian Journal of Gerontology*, 9(3-4) pp 1-10.

Prakash I.J., (2002), Overcoming Crisis in Care Giving— Strengthening 'Familism' in India, Emerging Trends and Perspectives, Hyderabad Heritage Hospital, pp 26-32.

Prakash I.J., (2003), (ed) Aging - Emerging Issues, Bangalore University.

Patil G.D, Patil M.D. and Sunil Kumar, D., (1991), Impact of Aging on Life Satisfaction of Elderly Women; in Prakash I.J. (ed) *Quality Aging—Collected Papers*, Varanasi Association of Gerontology, India, pp 141-150.

Pinto, A Life quality of the aged: Elderly Care at Home and Institution; in Prakash I.J. (ed) *Quality Aging, Collected Papers*, Varanasi Association of Gerontology, India, pp 162-168.

Rao A.V., (1997) Psychiatric Morbidity in the Aged, *Indian Journal of Medical Research*, 106, pp 376-380.

Singh R.R., (1995), Family Change – elder Care Needs and Social Policy in V.Kumar (ed) *Aging Indian Perspectives and Global Scenario*, New Delhi, AIIMS, pp 171-177.

Sreenivas M, (1999), The Psychological Quality of Post-retirement Life of Sports Person; Unpublished Ph.D thesis, Bangalore University, Bangalore.

Vijay Kumar S., (1997), Aging in India –Overview, *Indian Journal of Medical Research*, 106, pp 257-264.

Select Presentations and Discussion

Dr Lakshmidhar Mishra the then Secretary in the Union Ministry of Labour in his keynote address said that oldage was an important phase in the life cycle of a man. Every person had to go through that stage sooner or later. and face the consequences. Oldage is painful. As one grows older he or she is confined indoors with little or no mobility, cut off from the world outside. One is able to work less, produce less and earn less and therefore one needs an alternative secure source of income to see one sail through the stormy sea of life. The society had a moral obligation to assure them a life of dignity The workers who built the modern temples and ran the wheels of industry had a right to expect something in return from the society.

But as the world's population was ageing, the formal as well the informal arrangements for their upkeep were weakening and the aged people were losing the sense of security In the past the elderly were looked after by the family but the joint family system, the storehouse of love and affection, was breaking down, disappearing. Whatever income they had was losing its value due to inflation and new pressures, stresses and strains were being unleashed every day. They were suffering from poverty, deprivation and exclusion. left the world of work ingloriously, unseen and unheard.

In the circumstances the State should develop a new system of oldage security. The State is the agent of the society and it is incumbent on it to take cognisance of the inevitability of oldage and its dependence on the younger of sections society and to male appropriate provisions for the welfare of the aged including financial security, health security long term care, housing, recreation and other needs. Dr Mishra indicated that the new system of social security for the elderly should consist of three pillars: a publicly managed system with mandatory participation, a privately managed mandatory savings system and voluntary savings system.

Ms. Mary Johnson, the then Director, Area Office, International Labour Organisation, in her inaugural address drew attention to the changes occurring in the traditional background of the countries in the Asian sub Region resulting in the marginalisation of the elderly. She pointed out that due to the increase in life expectancy. the period of post retirement life was expected to become equal to the period of working life and therefore it had become essential for every one to make plans for long term post retirement life.

Ms. Johnson observed that the number of people covered under social security schemes in South Asian countries was very small and therefore it was necessary to evolve appropriate measures for extending the scope of social security schemes in order that the vulnerable sections of the society did not become more vulnerable. She offered the services of the ILO for formulating appropriate policies of social protection.

Mr Manfred Haack, Resident Representative of Friedrich Ebert Stiftung, a German Foundation, said that the system of social security in Germany and other Western Countries was built on the basis of solidarity among different sections of the people but that was breaking down in the wake of globalization. He expressed the view that an alternative system of cooperation needed to be developed whereby all members of the society at the global level could have social, economic, political security including health and legal security.

Mr. Dalial Uddin Mondal, Joint Secretary in the Ministry of Labour and Employment in the Government of Bangladesh stated that traditionally, the responsibility for the welfare of the elderly lay with their children and the State had virtually no obligation to provide for the elderly The kind of social security system obtaining in many of the high income countries was not a viable option for Bangladesh. However, Government employees at all levels enjoyed pension gratuity and other benefits after their retirement. The Government of Bangladesh had introduced a scheme of elderly allowance called Boyoskoo Bhata.and a scheme of oldage homes. He gave a brief description of the Schemes.

Mr. Zhang Guo Qing of the Ministry of Labour and social Security, China, presented a paper on Social Security for the Elderly in China. He said that since 1950's, the elderly protection had been emphasized in a series of laws. Lately, China was transforming from family care to social security in terms of support to the elderly but the transition would take a long period of time considering the traditional culture and economic development. In view of the transition to a market economy, population migration and more opportunities of women employment, the current emphasis was on community-based services.

The community care policies were first launched in the late of 1980's. In the past years, through the mixed efforts by the local community assistance and government action there were 0.93 million community care establishments, 5,055 community service centers and 1.01 million residents convenience stations set up all over the nation. Among them 85% facilities were available to provide services for the elderly. The main care giving programs from the community care system were as follows:

1. Daily care services: Including repair of household appliances, tailoring, haircutting, meals, housework, shopping and assistance in communicating with family members;

2. Health care: Medical care, physical check-up, emergency service and rehabilitation;

Home clinic, regular and irregular mobile out patient service, home consulting, family hospital beds provision and mutual cooperative health program in rural areas;

3. Cultural activities: Entertainment including old-age fashion show and dancing, TV and newspaper, chess and cards;

Life-long learning program with 13, 000 Old-age Universities to provide English language, computer, history, family education, calligraphy, painting and cooking courses for their more than 1 million elderly students.

4. Reemployment service: Providing job development, job counseling and job placement to help the younger elderly more employable.

Mr. Parduman Singh, President of the Social Security Association of India, presenting a paper on "Social Security for the Elderly in India" said that during the two centuries of British rule pension scheme was introduced for government employees only. and no other section of the population was covered even under a provident fund scheme what to say of pension scheme. After Independence the national government introduced the Caol Mines Provident fund Scheme and the Employees Provident Fund Scheme but there was no pension scheme for nearly 50 years until the Employees Pension Scheme was introduced on his own initiative. It was followed by several other occupational pension schemes. At the same time a National Oldage Pension Scheme was also introduced for the benefit of destitute old people of the age of 65 or more. Setting uniform standards for the oldage pension schemes which were prevalent in some of the States.

Mr. Singh then referred to what he called the dangerous tends in income protection for the elderly and expressed the view that they should be avoided.

The first such trend was the recommendation of the World Bank in favour of a three tier system. Mr. Singh said that the thesis on which the recommendations had made was entirely wrong.

The second trend was the enactment of laws in China and some States in India making it obligatory for the children to support the elderly. Mr. Singh expressed the view that such laws would not solve the problem.

The third trend was the recommendation of a Committee (Dave Committee) for introduction of individual retirement accounts. Mr. Singh said that the recommendation was totally unrealistic.

Mr. Singh said that these trends were a negation of the concept of social security according to which the society as a whole must look after the aged through social assistance schemes financed from tax revenues. He also made several suggestions for health security of the aged people and for providing them shelter.

Mr. K.C.Bahadur, Ministry of Labour in the Government of Nepal stated that traditionally, the society including the extended joint family system and the community had performed the role of the social security providers in Nepal. But the responsibility was gradually shifting to the State. Mr. Bahadur pointed out that the law relating to Government employees provided for payment of pension on retirement from service, the maximum pension being 50 per cent of the pay last drawn. In the case of industrial labour there was provision of provident fund. The employers as well as the employees contributed to the provident fund 10 per cent of the wages payable to the workers. They were also entitled to gratuity. Other indigent people were paid an allowance for their subsistence; Government was running an oldage home in Kathmandu and giving assistance to several NGOs running such homes. Government had drawn up a draft policy for the elderly people.

Mr. Boralugoda Sirisena of Sri Lanka stated that there was a broad social security system operating in Sri Lanka consisting of the following schemes:

Public Service Pension Scheme (PSPS)

Public Servants Provident fund Scheme (PSPF)
Local government Officers Pension Scheme (LGOPS)
Employees Provident Fund
Employees Trust Fund
Farmers Pension Scheme/Fishermen's Pension Scheme

Mr Sirisena observed that, in general, most of the elderly in Sri Lanka as in other countries in South Asia, did not depend on the formal system of income support in oldage but largely on the family network. He anticipated that even the existing pension schemes would face the problem of the rising costs.

Dr. Vijay Kumar of the Council for Social Development, (India) presented a paper on Issues of Aging in India: After describing the current situation of social security for the elderly in India he made certain critical observations about the existing schemes and drew attention to the grey areas which needed to be attended and suggested a plan of future action. In conclusion Dr Vijay Kumar stated that the Welfare State ideology was no longer suitable for the welfare of the elderly He felt that the Welfare State model should yield to a Welfare Community model in which apart from the State itself Social Action Groups, and other community organizations, the members of the family and the individuals themselves would be involved in drafting and implementing programmes for the welfare of the elderly. He suggested that a New National Policy for the Welfare of the Elderly should be evolved accordingly.

Mr. A.N. Roy, the former Additional Central Provident Fund Commissioner, (India) presented a paper on the Employees Pension Scheme, 1996 in India. He gave a brief account of the history and the salient features of the Scheme and addressed some of the criticisms against the Scheme.

Mr. G.N. Agarwal, Secretary (Pension and Groups Schemes) of the Life Insurance Corporation of India presented a paper on the role of the LIC in providing Income Security to the Elderly and gave a brief description of all the pension schemes introduced by the LIC. Explaining the rationale of the schemes he observed that investment planning was essential to ensure adequate income after retirement when income from work would stop .While a person could take risks during his working life any misadventure in making investments meant for post retirement life would be disastrous as one might be left with little or no financial asset or income. He pointed out according to the economic theory the aim of every individual would be to use his assets in such a way as would maximize happiness. As per the Permanent Income Hypothesis it would involve having similar amounts of income for spending, in real terms, each year. Thus the amount of money that a person would invest/disinvest would be what was necessary to convert his variable income stream into a level expenditure stream. Such an equation of income and expenditure could be achieved through a superannuation or annuity scheme.

Dr. Vinod Kumar, former Head, Geriatric Clinic of AIMS New Delhi spoke about health security and long term care of the elderly. He said that several factors operated over different stages of a man's life to promote healthy ageing. Of these some had a positive and the others negative bearing on the problem. Positive factors included physical activity, healthy diets, absence of alcohol and tobacco abuse, active social cultural activities and good family support. Negative factors included poor hygiene, low socio economic status, illiteracy, mental stress etc. Genetic and gender related factors also influenced the human life span and onset some of the chronic diseases.

Dr. Kumar went on to say that over the years health care had become expensive but it was not the financial capability alone which determined the delivery of health care. Attitudes and perceptions of people were also important. Economic constraints, coupled with illiteracy, insensitivity and lack of public awareness are some of the impediment to proper health care.

There were no separate health care services for older persons in India Lately, Government had started supporting mobile medicare, day care and oldage home services for the older persons. Nevertheless, health delivery knowledge and skills, in rural geriatric care had not been accorded due attention so far. An important aspect of the health care delivery to older persons was deficient utilization of available services. Main reasons for under-utilisiation of the services were inaccessibility due to distance, lack of escort, immobility, ignorance and poverty.

Dr. Vinod Kumar said that many NGOs were delivering health care service to the aged people. Some were providing outreach services and organizing medical camps in their local areas of operation Eye camps were particularly popular. Many NGOs were giving assistance to the needy people by supplying eye glasses, hearing and other aids free of cost.[1]

Dr. Kumar suggested revamping of the primary health care system and introduction of the systems of managed care and development of health insurance in the private sector.

Mr. A Prakash Rao of the Institute of Social and Economic Change presented a paper on the kind of support required by different categories of Elderly. He spoke about a study conducted by him in Karnataka and the findings of the study. Which were as follows:

The needs of the aged vary across gender, age, socio economicstrata and living status, whether living with family or outside, .The needs of the aged in oldage homes differed substantially from those who lived with their families.

The needs of the aged among general population differed from those belonging to deprived groups.

There existed gender differences across the needs and the support system aspired for by the aged people irrespective of the place where they lived.

Sri Prakash Rao said that the aged should be considered as a valuable human resource and utilization of the resource should be well planned.Intervention strategies should cover the entire span of life of the individual As women often outlived men greater attention should be given to the female older persons. Traditional Indian values of love and respect for the elderly should be actively promoted.

Concluding Remarks

Mr. John Woodall presiding over the concluding session of the Seminar said that there were three ideas behind the Seminar, namely, (a) to identify the role and responsibilities of the ILO in promoting social security (b) to consolidate the experiences of experts in the South Asian sub-region; and (c) to establish a foundation for some kind of practical action in the future. A technical team of the ILO was providing useful information and guidelines to social security experts in the sub region according to the needs of the respective countries. Lately the ILO was stressing on four themes: right to work, employment promotion social protection and social dialogue. Any discussion on social security should be appreciated in the light of their bearing on these complementary themes.

Mr. Woodall said that the world was in a state of flux and many things were changing. People should be ready to adapt themselves to the changing times and circumstances. One should anticipate the problems that might arise in the future and be ready with the solutions to those problems.

Mr. Woodall said that there was a psychological dimension to the problem of social security and that could be met only by bringing the traditional social safety nets provided by the community and the family to the mainstream.

Mr. Ravindra Verma delivering the valedictory address said that the world was faced with a challenge of the increasing numbers of graying population and each country was developing its own strategy to cope with it. But it could not be said that any of them was totally successful. The elderly persons had made their contribution to the community when they were young and it was now the duty of the community to look after them and to ensure that they got their due share of the fruits of development. It was therefore necessary for the community to evolve appropriate policies and programmes of social security for the elderly whereby the basic needs of the elderly could be met. In their case income security was not enough. They need ed, apart from adequate income, good health care, proper shelter and emotional security. In fact they needed psychological security more than anything else. The biggest question an elderly person faced at this time was on whom to depend the family or the State. In the wake of globalization neither the family nor the State was in a position to take care of the elderly. It was therefore necessary to evolve a new institutional framework for the upkeep of the aged persons.

Notes

1. The Mobile Medical Units of Helpage India is a notable example of such service provided by NGOs. The first mobile medical unit was started in 1982. Since then many more units have been set up. It is reported that there are at present 44 mobile medical units being run by Helpage India providing a wide range of services, namely, preventive healthcare and counseling medical check ups, medication to treat the most common ailments.

Maintaining Quality of Life for Elderly (Conclusion)

R.KA. SUBRAHMANYA

Oldage is an important phase in the life cycle of a man. Every person has to go through that stage sooner or later and face the consequences. Oldage is painful. As one grows older he or she is confined indoors with little or no mobility, cut off from the world outside. One is able to work less, produce less and earn less and therefore one needs an alternative secure source of income to see one sail through the stormy sea of life. The society has a moral obligation to assure the elderly a life of dignity. The workers who built the modern temples and ran the wheels of industry have a right to expect something in return from the society in their oldage.

Oldage is a contingency which is certain to come about and society should make relevant provision for its senior citizens on an equally assured basis. There are several aspects to this question. Economic and financial considerations are extremely important but it is inappropriate that they should be allowed to dictate the philosophical or constitutional basis on which a country chooses to make social provisions of this kind.

As the world's population is ageing, the formal as well the informal arrangements for their upkeep are weakening and the aged people are losing the sense of security In the past the elderly were looked after by the family but the joint family system, the storehouse of love and affection, is breaking down, disappearing. Whatever income they have is losing its value due to inflation and new pressures, stresses and strains are being unleashed every day. They are suffering from poverty, deprivation and exclusion.

The family as a single unit is likely to change. The oldage dependency would increase faster than the decline in child dependency. It would require lot of adjustment at the family level to accommodate and care for the elderly. While the daughters and daughters-in-law are replacing their role as care-givers to their parents by working outside home, a new challenge for the elderly care would be posed.

Day care centres, geriatric hospitals and oldage homes are likely to play major roles in the living arrangements for the elderly.

The elderly are likely to become more vulnerable in the absence of familial support network; hence they need a strong social security system. The current elderly who have not made adequate provision for oldage might be in for a great deal of frustration at the hands of their children during the oldage. Social security measures for the prospective elderly would thus become imperative.

In the circumstances the State should develop a new system of oldage security. The State is the agent of the society and it is incumbent on it to take cognisance of the inevitability of oldage and its dependence on the younger of sections society and to make appropriate provisions for the welfare of the aged including financial security, health security, long term care, housing, recreation and other needs.

Over the years different facets of social security provision have been developed but there are a number of issues yet to be settled. These issues have been cast in the form of a worldwide debate as to the affordability of social security for oldage, particularly in the current context of globalization, liberalization and informalisation of the labour market. Many commentators have come to the conclusion that pension reform is necessary and this has had an impact on the development of policies towards social security and social protection. Much of the arguments advanced in favour of pension reforms reflected muddled thinking. Social security schemes are not created in a social vacuum and they should not be viewed simply as the vehicles for financial and investment purposes. They are designed to provide appropriate support for those whose ability to generate their own income is lost. If this is taken as a fundamental premise the details of policy regarding oldage security could be developed in a logical and coherent manner taking into account the prevailing conditions of the country.

The starting point for establishing a national policy for the elderly is to regard them as full members of the society and to establish a national commitment to provide for them as a matter of right, and on the basis of the contribution they had already made to society through their working lifetimes. The need to provide pensions should be recognized as a long term commitment. The elderly should be seen as entitled to an appropriate share of national income and the real value of that share should be protected against inflation preferably on an income related rather than price determined basis.

It is a time of change, the impact of which could be felt with great strength on social provisions for the elderly members of each nation's society. In the past, support for this segment of society reflected long held values, notably of respect, entrenched in national cultures. In the frenetic pacc of modern, increasingly urban, lifestyles, it is easy for such values to be overlooked but it is important that they should not be forgotten or extinguished. Newer values of solidarity, which might buttress or substitute family and kinship ties, are also under pressure in materialistic societies, but must also be maintained and reinforced. All round the world, societies face difficult adjustments to face economic trends of globalization, urbanisation and increasingly informal or unorganized modes of employment and the demographic trends which are leading to dramatically increased dependency ratios. The need to balance the claims of dependent segments of population with those of the producers of current wealth and income demanded clear analysis and leadership from the leaders of society. Every one would become old in due course and would hope to live out a ripe oldage in conditions of financial comfort however modest. This reflection should guide the manner in which the problems of those who have already reached that seniority are addressed.

Lately, China was transforming from family care to social security in terms of support to the elderly but the transition would take a long period of time considering the traditional culture and economic development. In view of the transition to a market economy, population migration and more opportunities of women employment, the current emphasis was on community-based services.

The Welfare State ideology is no longer suitable for the welfare of the elderly. The Welfare State model should yield to a Welfare Community model in which apart from the State itself Social Action Groups, and other community organizations, the members of the family and the individuals themselves would be involved in drafting and implementing programmes for the welfare of the elderly. A New National Policy for the Welfare of the Elderly should be evolved accordingly.

Investment planning is essential to ensure adequate income after retirement when income from work would stop. While a person could take risks during his working life any misadventure in making investments meant for post-retirement life would be disastrous as one might be left with little or no financial asset or income. According to the economic theory the aim of every individual would be to use his assets in such a way as would maximize happiness. As per the

Permanent Income Hypothesis it would involve having similar amounts of income for spending, in real terms, each year. Thus the amount of money that a person would invest/disinvest would be what was necessary to convert his variable income stream into a level expenditure stream. Such an equation of income and expenditure could be achieved through a superannuation or annuity scheme.

The new system of social security for the elderly should consist of three pillars—a publicly managed system with mandatory participation, a privately managed mandatory savings system and voluntary savings system.

The number of people covered under social security schemes in South Asian countries is very small and therefore, it is necessary to evolve appropriate measures for extending the scope of social security schemes in order that the vulnerable sections of the society do not become more vulnerable.

There is a growing demand for pension from different classes of people but the pension market has not been properly tapped. The pension market potential in India is very vast but very little had been done to tap it. Providing for pension by saving all through one's working life time necessarily implies availability of long term and relatively safe investment avenues. But in India the long term debt market has not developed well. Equity market is highly volatile and ownership of property is fraught with legal hurdles. Further very high rates of inflation has discouraged people from sacrificing present consumption for the sake of a meagre post-retirement income in terms of its purchasing power. Unlike the developed countries where the pension system is built on a comprehensive state pension provision forming part of the social security net. India did not have any significant State Pension framework for the population as a whole. In such a situation it is difficult for anyone to maintain the same standard of living in oldage as during the working life. The following reform measures are necessary steps for developing the pension market:

- the first step is to liberalise portfolio allocation rules;
- the second step is to provide for an increased role for private pension management; and
- the third step is to create awareness among the public to avoid oldage crisis in future.

The World Bank's Multi Pillar framework enunciated in its report "Averting the Oldage Crisis" (1994) has had an important impact on recent thinking about pension reform. Among the three pillars suggested by the World Bank, the second pillar, i.e., privately (or publicly) managed mandatory savings pillar has received the most attention as it has been the main component of pension reform in Chile, and other parts of Latin America as well as some OECD countries. This has been the primary pillar in Singapore and Malaysia and its importance is growing in Indonesia and Thailand. The main thrust of the OASIS (Dave Committee) has also been towards making this pillar more effective and efficient in the Indian context. It is this pillar which is expected to shoulder the main burden of providing retirement protection. At the same time, the importance of the defined benefit, PAYG pillar is being reduced over time. It is recognized that to ensure creditability and support this reduction should not be at the expense of those who have accumulated pension benefits under the current systems. How to finance the accumulated benefits under the DB, PAYG systems, while simultaneously moving to the second pillar is an important design issue. Strong fiscal position, as well as well functioning banking system and the capital markets could by easing tensions help address the issue. Countries like India with weak position could not afford to unduly delay this transition as longer the delay the greater would be the fiscal burden. The following minimum conditions for a credible and sustainable pension reform are necessary in the formal sector in India:

- Stable and sustainable macro-economic framework.
- Adequate legal and financial sector regulatory framework.
- International benchmarking of business transparency and corporate governance.
- Investment diversification.
- Competition in pension fund management industry.

Health Care

The increasing number and proportion of elderly would have a direct impact on the demand for health services. Currently, the Government of India is running various health programmes targeted primarily at the needs of mothers and children. Primary health care system is not geared up to meet the future challenges arising from an increase in chronic diseases. Conditions like hypertensions and diabetes, which have higher incidence among the aged, would pose an increasing burden to the elderly themselves and to their families. Mobilising additional resources for geriatric care would emerge as a major responsibility of healthcare providers in countries like India. Achieving this without affecting maternal and pediatric care will be a challenge.

Several factors operated over different stages of a man's life to promote healthy ageing. Of these, some have a positive and the others negative bearing on the problem. Positive factors included physical activity, healthy diets, absence of alcohol and tobacco abuse, active social cultural activities and good family support. Negative factors include poor hygiene, low socio-economic status, illiteracy, mental stress etc. Genetic and gender related factors also influenced the human life span and onset of some of the chronic diseases.

Over the years health care has become expensive but it is not the financial capability alone which determines the delivery of health care. Attitudes and perceptions of people are also important. Economic constraints, coupled with illiteracy, insensitivity and lack of public awareness are some of the impediment to proper health care.

There are no separate health care services for older persons in India. Lately, Government has started supporting mobile medicare, day care and oldage home services for the older persons. Nevertheless, health delivery knowledge and skills, in rural geriatric care has not been accorded due attention so far. An important aspect of the health care delivery to older persons is deficient utilization of available services. Main reasons for under-utilisiation of the services are inaccessibility due to distance, lack of escort, immobility, ignorance and poverty.

Many NGOs are delivering health care service to the aged people. Some are providing outreach services and organizing medical camps in their local areas of operation. Eye camps are particularly popular. Many NGOs are giving assistance to the needy people by supplying eye glasses, hearing and other aids free of cost.[1]

It is necessary to revamp the primary health care system and introduce systems of managed care and develop health insurance in the private sector.

Many of the aged have mobility restrictions, dementia, medical problems and need assistance. As far as possible, older people should continue to be cared for by the community in family settings. A consensus is emerging for a holistic approach incorporating the assessment of physical and social functioning as well as the assessment of economic and environmental resources with due regard to the social independence status of the individuals. The factors that should be kept in view while planning the type of care required, are: household and personal care, mobility, mental state, physical environment and social environment. The options available depending on the needs of the individuals, namely, hospital, residential homes, special housing, day centres, day centres plus home helps, home nursing, home meals, etc. and ordinary housing with availability of static/mobile medical facilities.

In the coming decade the policy makers would have to evolve strategies for developing community based services with greater involvement of the participants and their families in planning and choosing the services and cited certain innovative approaches.

Maintenance of Quality of Life

The quest to maintain quality of life of older people usually focuses on economic security. However, health and emotional security are as important as economic security. The ingredients of psychological security could be broken down to some important components. People as they age need to feel wanted, useful, have autonomy and feel that their opinions are valued and respected. In pre-industrial societies a series of roles were generally reserved for the elderly people and those roles gave a sense of prestige to the persons. But such activities were no longer open to those who were caught up in the path of modernisation. In the past, the traditional structure of the life cycles, (ashrama dharma), structure of the family (joint family system), expertise in the respective occupations, control over resources, solidarity of the castes (biradri) etc. were the sources of psychological security. They have now disappeared resulting in the loss of meaningful roles to play in the family and the society, loss of social networks, loss of prestige, and status, obsolescence of the traditional knowledge and experience, and loss of control over economic resources etc. Dr Prakash expressed the view that family support was essential to counteract the negative elements in the life of he elderly and therefore families needed to be strengthened to care for the old.

While social security assures a decent living, emotional security makes it meaningful. Social security is essential to life at any age but psychological security is necessary for the aged to enable them to enjoy the benefits that economic security bestows. Social and emotional security together would add up to quality ageing.

The realization that the psychological factor should be considered in promoting active ageing has come with developments in Gerontology. This field is witnessing a paradigm shift. This involves a shift of focus from illness and disability associated with age to reserve capacity and preservation of competence; from frailty and dependence to positive health; from 'doing something for the elderly' attitude to people as partners in development; from a curative, rehabilitative approach to successful and productive ageing; from treating elderly as dependants who are served by society to acknowledging that elderly can plan, manage, and institute appropriate programmes for their own well being.[2]

The needs of the aged vary across gender, age, socio economic strata and living status, whether living with family or outside. The needs of the aged in oldage homes differed substantially from those who lived with their families.

The needs of the aged among general population differed from those belonging to deprived groups.

There existed gender differences across the needs and the support system aspired for by the aged people irrespective of the place where they lived.

The aged should be considered as a valuable human resource and utilization of the resource should be well planned. Intervention strategies should cover the entire span of life of the individual. As women often outlived men greater attention should be given to the female older persons. Traditional Indian values of love and respect for the elderly should be actively promoted.

Long Tem Care

With the growth of the population of the aged, the associated problem of caring for the aged is becoming increasingly important. Lately, long term care of the elderly in some of the developed countries has been systematized in the form of social care insurance as a part of social security. It has been reported that in 1991, in Germany, approximately one-third of the social security expenditures was devoted to care provision. The concept of care dependency is distinct from treatment for illness and covers help with daily tasks that do not fall under any medical treatment plan, e.g., personal hygiene, feeding, mobility or housework.

In the US there are many home health care agencies providing care for patients who do not need high level hospital care but still require part time nursing or physical therapy.

There may be terminally ill patients who cannot be cured of their maladies but need comfort so that thcy may die in peace. Hospices provide such care.

There are many voluntary organisations providing medical care as well as long term care and hospice care to the elderly in India but they are not adequate. Considering the size of the elderly population in India their care cannot be left entirely to voluntary organisations. The State has to come in big way and support private efforts so that they may expand their services.

Oldage Homes

This brings us to the next question relating to the shelter needs of the elderly. While ordinarily the elderly persons live with their children and grand children, circumstances are developing in such a way that many of them have had to live independently or under institutional care. Sometimes the health condition of the persons may be such that the concerned families may not be able to provide the necessary care. In some cases there may be no family at all. At the worst, the families might have abandoned them. The elderly persons would need institutional care in such circumstances. A WHO seminar of Health experts is reported to have concluded as follows:

> "The emergent need for some basic provision of institutional care is now evident in most countries of the region (Western Pacific countries). The seminar identified the need for Governments to take account of this trend to enact legislation and regulations to ensure good quality, appropriate, equitable, and cost-efficient provision of institutional services whether by the Government, non-Governmental organizations or the private sector".

The National Policy for Older Persons recognizes this need. The national policy is to consider institutional care as the last resort when personal circumstances are such that old age homes become absolutely necessary. The policy provides for giving assistance to voluntary organizations for construction and maintenance of oldage homes.

According to information available there are over 300 oldage homes in this country. Some of these are maintained by the State Governments and most are run by non-Government organizations with assistance from Government. There are also some institutions run by private charitable institutions without any assistance from Government. The total number of inmates in these institutions is about 15,000. Assuming that at least 1per cent of the aged require institutional care, facilities would have to be created for providing institutional care to about fifteen lakh persons. (It has been reported that nearly 5 per cent of the elderly live in institutions abroad). It is doubtful if voluntary organizations will come forward to set up so many oldage homes. There is therefore no alternative to the Central and State Governments taking the initiative to set up their own homes in sufficient numbers.

One cannot be content with the setting up of the homes. The quality of service provided in these homes needs to be monitored. The existing arrangements in this regard are less than adequate. It is therefore necessary to establish a well organised regulatory system to ensure that standards are maintained and exploitation avoided.

Emotional Support to the Elderly: Strengthening the Family System

Institutional care cannot be a total substitute for family care. The Committee on the Problems of the Aged referred to above made certain significant observations in this regard. The Committee observed:

" Aging is not only a physical process but also a state of mind. The physical process can be slowed down by advances in medical science and by keeping good health. The state of mind also affects the rate at which a person ages. A person is to a great extent, conditioned by how old he feels he is, rather than how old he actually he is. Such feelings are usually fostered by attitudes of society. Today, large sections of society still deem the elderly to be group of persons who should be classified with the sick and the disabled. Who are no longer fit for employment or capable of being retrained or reeducated to fit into new jobs. Such myths are often encouraged by media coverage of the elderly as weak and dependant. For, from being a burden, the elderly should be recognised as possessing experience, skills, knowledge, talent and wisdom, all of which are invaluable national assets. They should therefore not be isolated from the mainstream of society."

"Home for the aged can be built but experience all over the world has shown that this is not the kind of place where the elderly should be kept. The elderly need to remain active, to know that they still have a part to play in the family or community to which they can make a useful contribution. They still need to feel wanted and loved. To put them in institutions is to let them know that they are being discarded. The support and care must come from the heart, with feelings of sympathy affection and compassion. "The Committee had therefore recommended that concerted effort must therefore be made to preserve and strengthen the traditional family system. "Instead of admitting the elderly to institutions in the false hope that the problem will stop there, the government should adopt a national policy aimed at keeping every elderly individual physically and mentally fit and active so that he can retain his normal living arrangements as long as possible."

There can therefore no better way to provide the emotional support the elderly need as they grow older.

To sum up the elderly persons are a highly vulnerable group in society. Their vulnerability increases with age. The vulnerability lies mainly in lack of employment, financial insecurity, ill health and neglect by society. Any system of social security of the elderly should address all these vulnerabilities. It has therefore to be a multi-dimensional programme. providing income security, health security, long term care as well as emotional support. While the family can provide the basic security to the elderly the major responsibility for providing social security to the elderly lies on the community and the State.

Notes

1. The Mobile Medical Units of Helpage India is a notable example of such service provided by NGOs. The first mobile medical unit was started in 1982. Since then many more units have been set up. It is reported that there are at present 44 mobile medical units being run by Helpage India providing a wide range of services, namely, preventive healthcare and counseling medical check ups, medication to treat the most common ailments.
2. Role of Intergernational and Social Support in Active Ageing by Dr. Indira Jai Prakash; Active Ageing in the new Millinium edited by Aabha Choudhury, Anugraha, 2001.